THE KEY
STUDENT STUDY GUIDE

THE KEY student study guide is designed to help students achieve success in school. The content in each study guide is 100% curriculum aligned and serves as an excellent source of material for review and practice. To create this book, teachers, curriculum specialists, and assessment experts have worked closely to develop the instructional pieces that explain each of the key concepts for the course. The practice questions and sample tests have detailed solutions that show problem-solving methods, highlight concepts that are likely to be tested, and point out potential sources of errors. *THE KEY* is a complete guide to be used by students throughout the school year for reviewing and understanding course content, and to prepare for assessments.

Rao, Gautam, 1961 –

THE KEY – Mathematics 4

ISBN: 978-1-77044-435-5

1. Mathematics – Juvenile Literature. I. Title

Published by
Castle Rock Research Corp.
2000 First & Jasper
10065 Jasper Avenue
Edmonton, AB T5J 3B1

10 9 8 7 6

Publisher
Gautam Rao

Contributors
Phyllis Kozak

Dedicated to the memory of Dr. V. S. Rao

THE KEY — Math 4

THE KEY consists of the following sections:

KEY Tips for Being Successful at School gives examples of study and review strategies. It includes information about learning styles, study schedules, and note taking for test preparation.

Class Focus includes a unit on each area of the curriculum. Units are divided into sections, each focusing on one of the specific expectations, or main ideas, that students must learn about in that unit. Examples, definitions, and visuals help to explain each main idea. Practice questions on the main ideas are also included. At the end of each unit is a test on the important ideas covered. The practice questions and unit tests help students identify areas they know and those they need to study more. They can also be used as preparation for tests and quizzes. Most questions are of average difficulty, though some are easy and some are hard. Each unit is prefaced by a ***Table of Correlations***, which correlates questions in the unit to the specific curriculum expectations. Answers and solutions are found at the end of each unit.

KEY Strategies for Success on Tests helps students get ready for tests. It shows students different types of questions they might see, word clues to look for when reading them, and hints for answering them.

Practice Tests includes one to three tests based on the entire course. They are very similar to the format and level of difficulty that students may encounter on final tests. In some regions, these tests may be reprinted versions of official tests, or reflect the same difficulty levels and formats as official versions. This gives students the chance to practice using real-world examples. Answers and complete solutions are provided at the end of the section.

For the complete curriculum document (including specific expectations along with examples and sample problems), visit http://education.alberta.ca/media/645598/kto9math_ind.pdf.

THE KEY *Study Guides* are available for many courses. Check www.castlerockresearch.com for a complete listing of books available for your area.

For information about any of our resources or services, please call Castle Rock Research at 780.448.9619 or visit our website at http://www.castlerockresearch.com.

At Castle Rock Research, we strive to produce an error-free resource. If you should find an error, please contact us so that future editions can be corrected.

CONTENTS

KEY Tips for Being Successful at School

KEY TIPS FOR BEING SUCCESSFUL AT SCHOOL

KEY FACTORS CONTRIBUTING TO SCHOOL SUCCESS

In addition to learning the content of your courses, there are some other things that you can do to help you do your best at school. You can try some of the following strategies:

- **Keep a positive attitude**: Always reflect on what you can already do and what you already know.

- **Be prepared to learn**: Have the necessary pencils, pens, notebooks, and other required materials for participating in class ready.

- **Complete all of your assignments**: Do your best to finish all of your assignments. Even if you know the material well, practice will reinforce your knowledge. If an assignment or question is difficult for you, work through it as far as you can so that your teacher can see exactly where you are having difficulty.

- **Set small goals for yourself when you are learning new material**: For example, when learning the parts of speech, do not try to learn everything in one night. Work on only one part or section each study session. When you have memorized one particular part of speech and understand it, move on to another one. Continue this process until you have memorized and learned all the parts of speech.

- **Review your classroom work regularly at home**: Review to make sure you understand the material you learned in class.

- **Ask your teacher for help**: Your teacher will help you if you do not understand something or if you are having a difficult time completing your assignments.

- **Get plenty of rest and exercise**: Concentrating in class is hard work. It is important to be well-rested and have time to relax and socialize with your friends. This helps you keep a positive attitude about your schoolwork.

- **Eat healthy meals**: A balanced diet keeps you healthy and gives you the energy you need for studying at school and at home.

HOW TO FIND YOUR LEARNING STYLE

Every student learns differently. The manner in which you learn best is called your learning style. By knowing your learning style, you can increase your success at school. Most students use a combination of learning styles. Do you know what type of learner you are? Read the following descriptions. Which of these common learning styles do you use most often?

- Do you need to say things out loud? You may learn best by saying, hearing, and seeing words. You are probably really good at memorizing things such as dates, places, names, and facts. You may need to write down the steps in a process, a formula, or the actions that lead up to a significant event, and then say them out loud.

- Do you need to read or see things? You may learn best by looking at and working with pictures. You are probably really good at puzzles, imagining things, and reading maps and charts. You may need to use strategies like mind mapping and webbing to organize your information and study notes.

- Do you need to draw or write things down? You may learn best by touching, moving, and figuring things out using manipulatives. You are probably really good at physical activities and learning through movement. You may need to draw your finger over a diagram to remember it, tap out the steps needed to solve a problem, or feel yourself writing or typing a formula.

SCHEDULING STUDY TIME

You should review your class notes regularly to ensure that you have a clear understanding of all the new material you learned. Reviewing your lessons on a regular basis helps you to learn and remember ideas and concepts. It also reduces the quantity of material that you need to study prior to a test. Establishing a study schedule will help you to make the best use of your time.

- Regardless of the type of study schedule you use, you may want to consider the following suggestions to maximize your study time and effort:

- Organize your work so that you begin with the most challenging material first.

- Divide the subject's content into small, manageable chunks.

- Alternate regularly between your different subjects and types of study activities in order to maintain your interest and motivation.

- Make a daily list with headings like "Must Do," "Should Do," and "Could Do."

- Begin each study session by quickly reviewing what you studied the day before.

- Maintain your usual routine of eating, sleeping, and exercising to help you concentrate better for extended periods of time.

CREATING STUDY NOTES

MIND-MAPPING OR WEBBING

Use the key words, ideas, or concepts from your class notes to create a mind map or web, which is a diagram or visual representation of the given information. A mind map or web is sometimes referred to as a knowledge map. Use the following steps to create a mind map or web:

1. Write the key word, concept, theory, or formula in the centre of your page.

2. Write down related facts, ideas, events, and information, and link them to the central concept with lines.

3. Use coloured markers, underlining, or symbols to emphasize things such as relationships, timelines, and important information.

The following mind map is an example of one that could help you develop an essay:

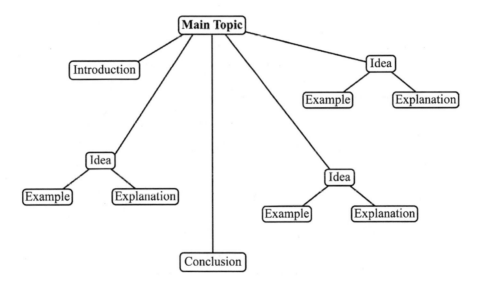

INDEX CARDS

To use index cards while studying, follow these steps:

1. Write a key word or question on one side of an index card.

2. On the reverse side, write the definition of the word, answer to the question, or any other important information that you want to remember.

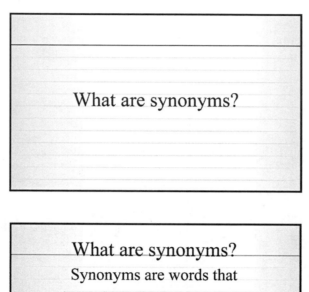

SYMBOLS AND STICKY NOTES—IDENTIFYING IMPORTANT INFORMATION

Use symbols to mark your class notes. For example, an exclamation mark (!) might be used to point out something that must be learned well because it is a very important idea. A question mark (?) may highlight something you are not certain about, and a diamond (◊) or asterisk (*) could highlight interesting information that you want to remember. Sticky notes are useful in the following situations:

• Use sticky notes when you are not allowed to put marks in books.

• Use sticky notes to mark a page in a book that contains an important diagram, formula, explanation, or other information.

• Use sticky notes to mark important facts in research books.

MEMORIZATION TECHNIQUES

The following techniques can help you when you need to memorize something:

- **Association** relates new learning to something you already know. For example, to remember the spelling difference between dessert and desert, recall that the word *sand* has only one *s*. So, because there is sand in a desert, the word *desert* has only one *s*.

- **Mnemonic** devices are sentences that you create to remember a list or group of items. For example, the first letter of each word in the phrase "**E**very **G**ood **B**oy **D**eserves **F**udge" helps you to remember the names of the lines on the treble-clef staff (E, G, B, D, and F) in music.

- **Acronyms** are words that are formed from the first letters or parts of the words in a group. For example, RADAR is actually an acronym for Radio Detecting and Ranging, and MASH is an acronym for Mobile Army Surgical Hospital. HOMES helps you to remember the names of the five Great Lakes (Huron, Ontario, Michigan, Erie, and Superior).

- **Visualizing** requires you to use your mind's eye to "see" a chart, list, map, diagram, or sentence as it is in your textbook or notes, on the chalkboard or computer screen, or in a display.

- **Initialisms** are abbreviations that are formed from the first letters or parts of the words in a group. Unlike acronyms, an initialism cannot be pronounced as a word itself. For example, BEDMAS is an initialism for the order of operations in math (Brackets, Exponents, Divide, Multiply, Add, Subtract).

KEY STRATEGIES FOR REVIEWING

Reviewing textbook material, class notes, and handouts should be an ongoing activity. Spending time reviewing becomes more critical when you are preparing for a test. You may find some of the following review strategies useful when studying during your scheduled study time:

- Before reading a selection, preview it by noting the headings, charts, graphs, and chapter questions.

- Before reviewing a unit, note the headings, charts, graphs, and chapter questions.

- Highlight key concepts, vocabulary, definitions, and formulas.

- Skim the paragraph, and note the key words, phrases, and information.

- Carefully read over each step in a procedure.

- Draw a picture or diagram to help make the concept clearer.

KEY STRATEGIES FOR SUCCESS: A CHECKLIST

Reviewing is a huge part of doing well at school and preparing for tests. Here is a checklist for you to keep track of how many suggested strategies for success you are using. Read each question, and put a check mark (✓) in the correct column. Look at the questions where you have checked the "No" column. Think about how you might try using some of these strategies to help you do your best at school.

KEY Strategies for Success	Yes	No
Do you attend school regularly?		
Do you know your personal learning style—how you learn best?		
Do you spend 15 to 30 minutes a day reviewing your notes?		
Do you study in a quiet place at home?		
Do you clearly mark the most important ideas in your study notes?		
Do you use sticky notes to mark texts and research books?		
Do you practise answering multiple-choice and written-response questions?		
Do you ask your teacher for help when you need it?		
Are you maintaining a healthy diet and sleep routine?		
Are you participating in regular physical activity?		

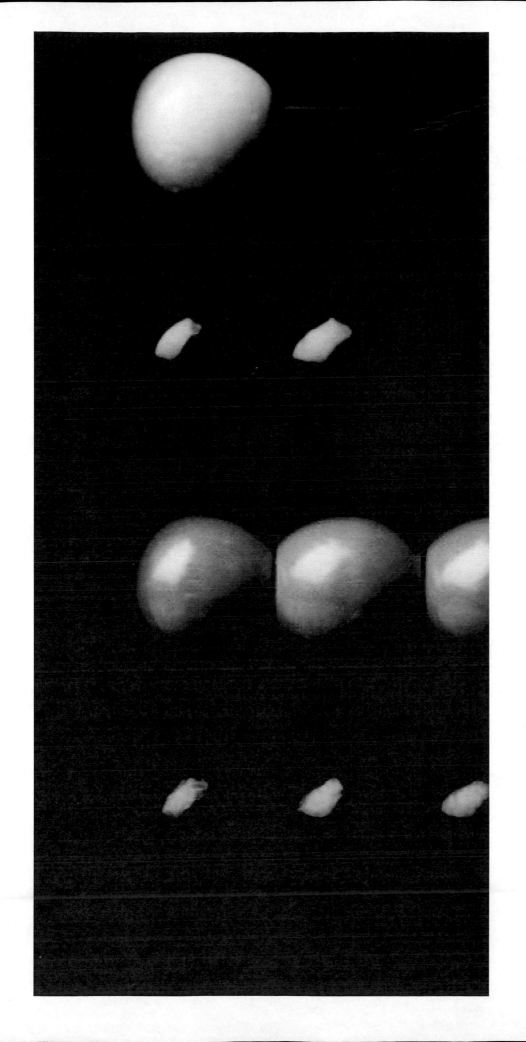

NUMBER

Table of Correlations

Outcome		Practice Questions	Unit Test Questions	Practice Test
4N1.0	Develop number sense			
4N1.1	Represent and describe whole numbers to 10 000, pictorially and symbolically.	1, 2, 3, 4, 5, 6, 7	1, 2, 3, 4, 5, 6, 7	1, 2
4N1.2	Compare and order numbers to 10 000.	8, 9, 10, 11, 12	8, 9, 10, 11	3, 4
4N1.3	Demonstrate an understanding of addition of numbers with answers to 10 000 and their corresponding subtractions (limited to 3- and 4-digit numerals).	13, 14, 15, 16, 17, 18	12, 13, 14, 15, 16, 17	5, 6
4N1.4	Apply the properties of 0 and 1 for multiplication and the property of 1 for division.	19, 20	18, 19	7
4N1.5	Describe and apply mental mathematics strategies for multiplication and division.	21, 22, 23	20, 21	8
4N1.6	Demonstrate an understanding of multiplication (2- or 3-digit by 1-digit) to solve problems.	24, 25, 26, 27, 28	22, 23, 24	9, 10
4N1.7	Demonstrate an understanding of division (1-digit divisor and up to 2-digit dividend) to solve problems.	29, 30, 31, 32, 33	25, 26, 27, 28	11
4N1.8	Demonstrate an understanding of fractions less than or equal to one by using concrete, pictorial and symbolic representations.	34, 35, 36, 37, 38, 39	29, 30, 31, 32, 33, 34	12, 13, 14
4N1.9	Represent and describe decimals (tenths and hundredths), concretely, pictorially and symbolically.	40, 41, 42, 43, 44, 45	35, 36, 37	15, 16, 17
4N1.10	Relate decimals to fractions and fractions to decimals (to hundredths).	46, 47, 48	38, 39	18
4N1.11	Demonstrate an understanding of addition and subtraction of decimals (limited to hundredths).	49, 50, 51, 52	40, 41, 42, 43	19

4N1.1 *Represent and describe whole numbers to 10 000, pictorially and symbolically.*

REPRESENTING AND DESCRIBING WHOLE NUMBERS

Whole numbers are digits (symbols) like 0, 1, 2, 3, 4, 5, 6, 7, 8, 9 and any combination of these digits. Whole numbers are used to count things, but not parts of things. Decimals, fractions, and negative numbers are not whole numbers.

- **Whole numbers:** 7, 63, 384, 9 501

- **Not whole numbers:** 0.5, 3.08, -7, $\frac{1}{4}$

When reading whole numbers with three or more digits, do not say the word *and* after the words *thousand* or *hundred*. For example, the number 4 732 is read as "four thousand seven hundred thirty-two".

Whole numbers can be represented and described using many methods.

USING BASE TEN MATERIALS

Base ten materials, like thousand cubes, hundred flats, ten rods, and units, can be used to represent whole numbers.

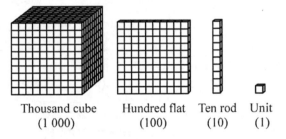

Thousand cube   Hundred flat   Ten rod   Unit
(1 000)   (100)   (10)   (1)

For example, the number 1 125 can be represented using the following base ten materials:

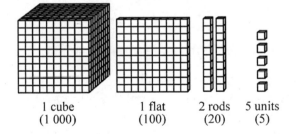

1 cube   1 flat   2 rods   5 units
(1 000)   (100)   (20)   (5)

USING PLACE VALUE AND PLACE VALUE CHARTS

Place value can be used to describe whole numbers. Place value tells you how much each digit in a number stands for (its value), according to its position in the number.

A **place value chart** is an organized method used to show the position or value of each digit in a number.

The following place value chart shows the positions and values of each digit in the number 9 326.

	Thousands	Hundreds	Tens	Ones
Position	9	3	2	6
Value	9 000	300	20	6

USING EXPANDED NOTATION

Expanded notation can be used to represent or describe whole numbers. Expanded notation is the sum of the place values of the digits in a number. For example, the expanded notation form of the number 5 432 is 5 000 + 400 + 30 + 2.

When you represent a number in expanded notation form, you do not need to include a place value of zero (0).

For example, the expanded notation form of the number 2 603 is usually written as 2 000 + 600 + 3.

USING WRITTEN FORM

Changing the numeric form of a numeral to its written form is another way to represent whole numbers. When writing four-digit numerals in written form, start with the number of thousands and continue writing the number of hundreds, tens, and ones.

Do not write the word *and* after the words *thousand* or *hundred*. Remember to use a hyphen (-) between the two digits for numbers between 21 and 99 that do not end in zero. For example, 21 is written as twenty-one.

Example

Caleb is asked to write the written form of the numeral 4 531. How should he write it?

To solve this problem, Caleb needs to remember to start with the digit in the thousands place and not to use the word *and*. To represent the number 4 531 in written form, Caleb should write "four thousand five hundred thirty-one".

USING NUMERIC (STANDARD) FORM

Any representation of a whole number can be written in numeric form. A four-digit **numeral** may be written with or without a space between the thousands and hundreds positions. For example, the number 1 803 can also be written as 1803.

When writing in numeric form, remember to use a digit for each place value. For example, 4 000 + 70 + 3 is written as 4 073 in its numeric form. The 0 saves the hundreds position.

1. Which of the following numerals represents the expanded notation
    5 000 + 200 + 40 + 3?

    A. 3 425   B. 5 234

    C. 5 243   D. 5 342

2. The expanded notation form of the numeral 3 042 is

    A. 3 + 0 + 4 + 2   B. 300 + 40 + 2

    C. 3 000 + 40 + 2   D. 3 000 + 400 + 2

3. What is the value of the digit 1 in the number 1 005?

    A. 1   B. 10

    C. 100   D. 1 000

4. Which of the following place value charts represents the number 7 113?

    A.
Thousands	Hundreds	Tens	Ones
7	0	11	3

    B.
Thousands	Hundreds	Tens	Ones
7	1	1	3

    C.
Thousands	Hundreds	Tens	Ones
7	11	0	3

    D.
Thousands	Hundreds	Tens	Ones
7	100	10	3

5. In the number 8 967, the value of the digit in the thousands place is

    A. 8 000   B. 8 900

    C. 8 960   D. 8 967

    Written Response

6. How can the numeral 3 534 be represented in written form?

Written Response

7. Explain the meaning of each digit in the number 9 872. You may use a chart or diagram to help you explain your answer.

4N1.2 *Compare and order numbers to 10 000.*

COMPARING AND ORDERING WHOLE NUMBERS

Two whole numbers can be compared. Once compared, the numbers can be ordered.

COMPARING NUMBERS

Compare two whole numbers to see which has:

- the greater value
- the lesser value
- equal (some) value

Use words or symbols to show the comparison of the numbers. When using symbols, you are comparing the first number on the left to the number that is on its right.

Example

- The number 5 000 is greater than 4 500.
  Using the greater than symbol, >, this can be shown as 5 000 > 4 500.
- The number 9 000 is less than 9 300.
  Using the less than symbol, <, this can be shown as 9 000 < 9 300.
- The number 10 000 is equal to 10 000.
  Using the = symbol, this can be shown as 10 000 = 10 000.

ORDERING NUMBERS

When ordering numbers from greatest value to least value, the numbers get smaller or lesser in value. This is called **descending order**.

For example, the following numbers are written in descending order: 3 890, 776, 345

When ordering numbers from least value to greatest value, the numbers get larger or greater in value. This is called **ascending order**.

For example, the following numbers are written in ascending order: 345, 776, 3 890

One strategy for comparing and ordering numbers is to write the numbers below each other, lining up the place values. Then start with the largest place value and compare the digits.

Example

Write the numbers 8 793, 8 973, and 8 397 in descending order.

Step 1
Write the numbers below each other, and line up the place values.
8 793
8 973
8 397

Step 2
Compare the thousands (largest place value).
Since all three numbers have the digit 8 in the thousands place, (8 thousands), move on to the hundreds place value.

Step 3
Compare the hundreds.
Since 9 > 7 and 7 > 3, then 8 973 > 8 793 and 8 793 > 8 397.
In descending order, the numbers are 8 973, 8 793, and 8 397.

USING NUMBER LINES

Number lines show the order of numbers.

:Example

Jan was asked to compare and order the numbers 4 190, 4 950, and 4 500 from least value to greatest value.

Jan used a number line that starts with 4 000 and ends with 5 000 to display the order of the three given numbers.

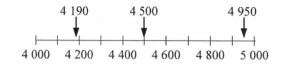

8. Which of the following sets of numbers is written in ascending order?
    A. 8 478, 8 200, 8 175   B. 8 478, 8 175, 8 200
    C. 8 175, 8 200, 8 478   D. 8 175, 8 478, 8 200

9. On which of the following number lines could the arrow represent the number 710?

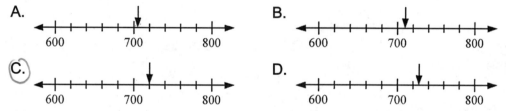

10. Janelle placed four sets of numbers in ascending order, but made an error in one of the sets.

    In which set of numbers did Janelle place a number **incorrectly**?

    A. 809, 909, 1 009, 1 109   B. 898, 998, 1 098, 1 198
    C. 908, 1 118, 1 108, 1 308   D. 993, 1 093, 1 193, 1 293

Use the following information to answer the next question.

Lois used arrows to show where she placed the numbers 3 695, 3 125, 3 050, and 3 955 on a number line.

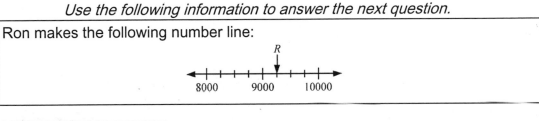

11. Which number did Lois place **incorrectly**?
 A. 3 050
 B. 3 125
 C. 3 695
 D. 3 955

Use the following information to answer the next question.

Ron makes the following number line:

$$R$$

8000   9000   10000

Numerical Response

12. What number does the letter *R* represent on Ron's number line? __9 100__

4N1.3 *Demonstrate an understanding of addition of numbers with answers to 10 000 and their corresponding subtractions (limited to 3- and 4-digit numerals).*

ADDITION AND SUBTRACTION OF 3- AND 4-DIGIT NUMBERS

STRATEGIES INVOLVING ADDITION AND SUBTRACTION

A **strategy** is a plan or a set of steps that helps you solve problems or do calculations quickly and easily. A personal strategy is a strategy that works best for you. The following are examples show strategies you can use when adding or subtracting.

USING STANDARD ALGORITHMS

A **standard algorithm** is a series of steps that you follow to add or subtract.

When you use a standard algorithm, it is important to line up the ones, tens, hundreds, and thousands. You begin the calculation at the right with the ones and move step-by-step to the left. You will need to regroup when necessary.

Example

Joe used an algorithm to solve this subtraction problem 5 732 – 2 413 = □

Step 1: Regroup the 3 tens and 2 ones into 2 tens and 12 ones.

```
    2 12
  5 7̶3̶2̶
 – 2 413
```

Step 2: Subtract the ones.

```
    2 12
  5 7̶3̶2̶
 – 2 413
        9
```

Step 3: Subtract the tens.

```
    2 12
  5 7̶3̶2̶
 – 2 413
       19
```

Step 4: Subtract the hundreds.

```
    2 12
  5 7̶3̶2̶
 – 2 413
      319
```

Step 5: Subtract the thousands.

```
    2 12
  5 7̶3̶2̶
 – 2 413
    3 319
```

USING PLACE VALUE AND EXPANDED NOTATION

For this strategy, you can break down the numbers into their place values and write the values in expanded notation form. You can then add or subtract the place values.

Example

Sam used place value and expanded notation to solve the addition problem 4 527 + 1 352 = □

4 527 = 4 000 + 500 + 20 + 7
1 352 = 1 000 + 300 + 50 + 2
          5 000 + 800 + 70 + 9 = 5 879

Using Estimation

Sometimes an exact answer is not needed, so an estimation can be made. An **estimate** gives you an approximate answer. The following three strategies can be used when estimating a sum or difference.

Rounding

When you round numbers, look at the number to the right of the number you are rounding.

If the number to the right is 5 or greater than 5, the number you are rounding goes up by one, and the numbers to the right are replaced with zeros.

For example, rounded to the nearest hundred, 4$\underline{7}$3 → 500.

If the number to the right is less than 5, the number you are rounding stays the same, and the numbers to the right are replaced with zeros.

For example, rounded to the nearest hundred, 3$\underline{2}$7 → 300.

Example

When asked to estimate the difference for the subtraction problem 152 – 73, Jill first rounded the numbers to the nearest ten.
152 → 150 and 73 → 70

She then subtracted the estimated numbers to get the estimated difference.
150 – 70 = 80

Front-End Estimation

When you use front-end estimation to estimate a sum or difference, you keep the front digits (the numbers with the greatest place values) and replace all the numbers to the right with zeros. You then add or subtract the estimated numbers.

Example

Reena uses front-end estimation to estimate the sum of 3457 + 1 562.
3 457 → 3 000 and 1 562 → 1 000

She then adds the estimated numbers to get an estimated sum.
3 000 + 1 000 = 4 000

Front-end estimated **sums** are always lower than the actual sums. Front-end estimated **differences** can be higher or lower than the actual difference.

:Example

Rakesh uses front-end estimation to esitmate the difference of 3 143 – 1 927.
3 143 → 3 000 and 1 927 → 1 000

He then subtracts the estimated difference.
3 000 – 1 000 = 2 000

Compensation

This strategy is very similar to front-end estimation. It is mainly used when estimating the sum of at least three numbers. Look at the first digit or the first two digits, but use the front digit +1 more for the last number.

:Example

Essa estimates the sum of 331 + 210 + 647.

He uses front-end estimation for the first two numbers and front end +1 more for the last number.
331 → 300, 210 → 200, and 647 → 700

He then adds the three estimated numbers to get an estimated sum.
300 + 200 + 700 = 1 200

SOLVING PROBLEMS INVOLVING ADDITION AND SUBTRACTION

When solving addition and subtraction problems, it is important to read the question carefully so you understand what is being asked. Pay close attention to key words. Words such as *total*, *in all*, *sum*, and *altogether* are clues that you probably need to add in order to solve the problem. Words like *more*, *fewer*, *not*, *difference*, and *left* are clues that you probably need to subtract.

USING INVERSE OPERATIONS

Addition and subtraction are opposite or inverse operations. You can check a subtraction question by using addition. You can check an addition question by using subtraction.

For example, if the problem is 175 – 125 = 50, the check is 50 + 125 = 175.

If the problem is 300 + 250 = 550, the check is 550 – 250 = 300.

Use the following information to answer the next question.

One of the mountains in Tibet is 7 553 m high. One of the mountains in Tanzania is 5 895 m high.

13. How much higher is the mountain in Tibet than the mountain in Tanzania?
    A. 1 658 m
    B. 1 758 m
    C. 2 658 m
    D. 2 768 m

Use the following information to answer the next question.

Jacob uses the strategy of expanded notation to help him subtract the two numbers in this problem:
2 651 – 1 320 = ☐

14. Which of the following expanded notations represents the solution to Jacob's problem?
    A. 3 000 + 900 + 70 + 1
    B. 2 000 + 600 + 50 + 1
    C. 1 000 + 300 + 30 + 1
    D. 1 000 + 300 + 20 + 0

15. In which of the following situations would an estimate rather than an exact answer be sufficient?
    A. Buying apples to make ten pies

    B. Taking cough syrup for your sore throat

    C. Buying enough stamps so you can mail a package

    D. Calculating the change you should receive after paying for a bag of chips.

Use the following information to answer the next question.

Conner collects sports cards. Right now, he has 4 562 cards in his collection. Conner then joins a club that will send him 100 cards each month for the next 6 months.

16. How many cards in total will Conner have at the end of 6 months?
    A. 4 662 cards
    B. 5 062 cards
    C. 5 162 cards
    D. 5 662 cards

Use the following information to answer the next question.

Jason needs to find the sum of 535 and 207 in order to solve a problem. He estimates the sum before he does the calculation.

17. The **best** estimate for the sum of 535 and 207 is
    A. 500
    B. 600
    C. 700
    D. 800

Use the following information to answer the next question.

Pam, Jon, and Mario each made an art picture out of sunflower seeds. Pam used 384 sunflower seeds, Jon used 422 sunflower seeds, and Mario used 516 sunflower seeds.

Numerical Response

18. Using front-end estimation, about how many sunflower seeds did Pam, Jon, and Mario use altogether? _____

4N1.4 *Apply the properties of 0 and 1 for multiplication and the property of 1 for division.*

PROPERTIES

The property of a number tells how that number will always affect the outcome of a solution.

PROPERTIES OF 0 AND 1 FOR MULTIPLICATION

The **property of 0 for multiplication** tells you that the product of any number and 0 is 0. No matter how large the number is, if it is multiplied by 0, the product will be 0.

$1 \times 0 = 0$
$2 \times 0 = 0$
$5 \times 0 = 0$
$10 \times 0 = 0$

The **property of 1 for multiplication** tells you that the product of any number and 1 is the number itself (the other number).

$3 \times 1 = 3$
$4 \times 1 = 4$
$5 \times 1 = 5$
$7 \times 1 = 7$

Remember that if $2 \times 1 = 2$, then $1 \times 2 = 2$.

Numerical Response

19. In the multiplication equation $80 \times 1 = A$, what number does the letter *A* represent?_____

Written Response

20. Solve this division problem:
    49 ÷ 1 = □

    Explain how the property of 1 for division can be applied to determine the answer to the division problem.

4N1.5 *Describe and apply mental mathematics strategies for multiplication and division.*

USING MENTAL STRATEGIES TO LEARN BASIC FACTS

Mental strategies are plans that can help you calculate quickly in your head. Following are some examples of mental strategies that may help you.

SKIP COUNTING FROM A KNOWN FACT

If you know that 3 × 1 = 3, you can skip count by 3s to find the product of 3 × 3.

3 × 1	3 × 2	3 × 3
3	6	9

DOUBLING, DOUBLING PLUS ONE GROUP, REPEATED DOUBLING

You can use easier facts to help you find the products of more difficult facts.

- **Doubling:** To multiply 4 × 6, think of 2 × 6 = 12, so 4 × 6 = 12 + 12 = 24.
- **Doubling plus one group:** To multiply 5 × 7, think of 5 × 6 = 30 and add one more group of 5, so 5 × 7 = 30 + 5 = 35
- **Repeated doubling:** To multiply 8 × 6, think of 2 × 6 = 12 and 4 × 6 = 24, so 8 × 6 = 24 + 24

HALVING, SUBTRACTING ONE GROUP

You can use facts you know to help you find the products of other facts.

- **Halving:** To multiply 4 × 8, think of 8 × 8 = 64.
  4 × 8 = 64 ÷ 2 = 32
- **Halving and subtracting one group:** To multiply 3 × 8, think of 8 × 8 = 64 and
  4 × 8 = 32 and then subtract one group of 8.
  3 × 8 = 32 – 8 = 24

RELATING DIVISION FACTS TO MULTIPLICATION FACTS

When you multiply two numbers, it does not matter in what order you place the numbers. The answer will be the same. For every fact that you learn, you can reverse the numbers and know two facts.
7 × 5 = 35 and 5 × 7 = 35

Since multiplication and division are opposite or inverse operations, you can use the same numbers and learn two division facts.

- If you know that 5 × 7 = 35, then you know that 35 ÷ 7 = 5.
- If you know that 7 × 5 = 35, then you know that 35 ÷ 5 = 7.

Two related multiplication facts and their two related division facts are often referred to as a **fact family**. If you know one of the facts, you actually know four facts: two multiplication facts and two division facts. You can use this strategy to determine the products or quotients of other facts.

Example

What two multiplication facts and two related division facts can describe this grouping of cookies?

Multiplication Facts	Related Division Facts
4 × 6 = 24	24 ÷ 6 = 4
6 × 4 = 24	24 ÷ 4 = 6

Use the following information to answer the next question.

Trish uses the mental strategy of "doubling and adding one more group" to solve a math fact.
$2 \times 8 = 16$ and $16 + 8 = 24$

21. Which of the following math facts was Trish solving?
    A. $8 \times 4 = K$ B. $3 \times 8 = K$
    C. $16 \div 2 = K$ D. $24 \div 4 = K$

Use the following information to answer the next question.

Raj uses the mental strategy of related multiplication facts to help him solve the division problem
$63 \div 9 = m$

22. Which of the following multiplication facts will help Raj solve the division problem?
    A. $6 \times 9 = m$

    B. $8 \times 9 = m$

    C. $9 \times 7 = m$

    D. $9 \times 9 = m$

Use the following information to answer the next question.

Kent used skip counting from a known fact to solve a multiplication problem.
… 18, 27, 36, 45, 54, 63

Numerical Response

23. By what number was Kent multiplying? _____

4N1.6 *Demonstrate an understanding of multiplication (2- or 3-digit by 1-digit) to solve problems.*

SOLVING PROBLEMS USING STRATEGIES FOR MULTIPLICATION

There are several strategies you can use to help you solve multiplication problems. The following are some strategies that you may find useful. Remember, a personal strategy is a strategy that works best for you.

USING ARRAYS

An **array** is a group of symbols or pictures arranged in columns and rows. It can also be the squares on a grid paper. You can use arrays to help you multiply.

Example

There are 12 eggs in one carton. Mrs. Brown bought 4 cartons.
How many eggs did Mrs. Brown buy altogether?

Step 1
Make the array.
Using grid paper, colour 12 squares in a row. Colour three more rows of squares right below the first row so that a rectangular shape is made.

Step 2
Determine the total number of eggs.
Add the number of squares in each row or multiply the number of rows by the number of squares in each row. Repeated addition is the same as multiplication.
12 + 12 + 12 + 12 = 48
12 × 4 = 48
Mrs. Brown bought a total of 48 eggs.

USING SYMBOLIC REPRESENTATIONS (NUMBERS)

You can use a standard algorithm to multiply. An algorithm is a set of steps you can follow when you calculate.

Example

Karen has 4 baskets of different coloured buttons. Each basket has 53 buttons. How many buttons does Karen have altogether?

To solve this problem, you need to multiply 53 by 4.

Step 1
Place the 2-digit number (53) above the 1-digit number (4) so that the ones line up.

$$\begin{array}{r} 53 \\ \times\ 4 \\ \hline \end{array}$$

Step 2
Multiply the ones. $3 \times 4 = 12$
Place the 2 ones (in 12) below the line.
Place the 1 ten (in 12) above the 5 tens.

$$\begin{array}{r} \overset{1}{5}3 \\ \times\ 4 \\ \hline 2 \end{array}$$

Step 3
Multiply the tens.
$4 \times 5 = 20$
Add the 1 ten that you carried to the tens place.
Place the 21 below the line, in front of the 2 ones.

$$\begin{array}{r} \overset{1}{5}3 \\ \times\ 4 \\ \hline 212 \end{array}$$

Karen has a total of 212 buttons.

CONNECTING CONCRETE AND SYMBOLIC REPRESENTATIONS

You can use place value and break down a larger number into hundreds, tens, and ones. Multiply the hundreds, tens, and ones separately by the same multiplier and then add the sums.

⁚Example

When the Grade Four class collected dimes for an animal shelter, they placed the dimes into 2 jars. Each jar held 225 dimes.
How many dimes did they collect in total?

You can use 2 hundred flats, 2 ten rods, and 5 units to represent the 225 dimes in each jar.

Step 1
Multiply the number of hundred flats, ten rods, and one units by 2.
200 × 2 = 400
20 × 2 = 40
5 × 2 = 10

Step 2
Add the sums.
400 + 40 + 10 = 450
The Grade Four class collected a total of 450 dimes.

ESTIMATING PRODUCTS

Sometimes you do not need an exact answer when solving a problem, or sometimes you might want to estimate an answer to see if your calculation is reasonable. You can estimate the numbers you are multiplying to get an "about" answer. You can use any estimation strategy that works for you. Some examples of estimation strategies are front-end estimation, compensation, and rounding.

Example

Jessie's mom used 3 packages of chocolate chips when she baked cookies for the school picnic. The labels on the packages said that there were at least 215 chips in each package.

About how many chocolate chips did Jessie's mom use?

Step 1
Round the number of chips using front-end estimation.
$215 \rightarrow 200$

Step 2
Multiply the estimated number of chips by the 3 packages.
$200 \times 3 = 600$
Jessie's mom used about 600 chocolate chips.

SOLVING PROBLEMS BY APPLYING THE DISTRIBUTIVE PROPERTY

The **distributive property** tells you that you can multiply each place value of a larger number by the multiplier and then add the products together. This is a strategy that can be used when multiplying large numbers.

Example

Kyle has four binders of hockey cards. Each binder has 145 cards. How many hockey cards does Kyle have altogether?

To solve this problem, you need to multiply 145 by 4.

Step 1
Rewrite the number 145 in expanded notation.
$145 = 100 + 40 + 5$

Step 2
Multiply each place value by 4.
$(100 \times 4) + (40 \times 4) + (5 \times 4)$
$= 400 + 160 + 20$

Step 3
Add the products.
$= 400 + 160 + 20$
$= 580$

:Example

Kassie is planning to go on a seven-day cruise to the Caribbean with her family. She visits a travel agency to obtain information on how much the cruise will cost. The cost for a room with a balcony on the cruise is $1 500 per person. The cost of a flight to the city where the cruise sets sail is $250 per person.

What is the total cost of the trip if 4 people from her family will be going on the cruise and will want their own room?

There are two methods that Kassie can use to figure out the answer to this problem.

Method 1

Find the total cost of one trip.
$1 500 + $250 = $1 750

Multiply the total cost of one trip by the number of people taking the trip (4).
$1 750 × 4 = $7 000

Method 2

Multiply the cost of the airfare (250) by the number of people taking the trip (4).
$250 × 4 = $1 000

Multiply the cost of the cruise ($1 500) by the number of people taking the trip (4).
$1 500 × 4 = $6 000.

Add the calculated values together.
$1 000 + $6 000 = $7 000

The distributive property says that these two methods should give the same result.
4(1 500 + 250) = 4(250) + 4(1 500)

To show this is true, calculate the result for each method. Remember to perform operations in the order given by BEDMAS; in this case, brackets first, then multiplication, and addition last.
$$4(1\ 500 + 250) = 4(250) + 4(1\ 500)$$
$$4 × 1\ 750 = 1\ 000 + 6\ 000$$
$$7\ 000 = 7\ 000$$

The total cost of the trip for all 4 people in Kassie's family will be $7 000.

---

24. Ali and Miyu were building bridges out of straws. They each built two bridges. Each bridge was made out of 212 straws.

    About how many straws in total did Ali and Miyu use?

    A. 1 000   B. 950

    C. 800   D. 750

25. One strategy that can be used to solve the multiplication problem 3 × 110 is
    A. (3 × 1) + (3 × 10)   B. (3 × 11) + (3 × 0)
    C. (3 × 101) + (3 × 0)   D. (3 × 100) + (3 × 10)

Use the following information to answer the next question.

A passenger train has 5 cars. Each car has 2 rows of seats and each row has 16 seats.

26. If 2 passengers sit on every seat, what is the **greatest** number of passengers that the train can carry?

    A. 320   B. 300

    C. 240   D. 160

Use the following information to answer the next question.

Multiplication facts can be represented by arrays.

27. Which of the following multiplication facts can represent the given array?

    A. $6 \times 14 = 78$ B. $6 \times 14 = 84$

    C. $7 \times 14 = 78$ D. $7 \times 14 = 98$

Numerical Response

28. For her birthday, Liza got 3 sticker books that each have 16 pages. There are spots on each page for 8 stickers to be pasted. How many stickers would be needed to fill all three books? _____

4N1.7 *Demonstrate an understanding of division (1-digit divisor and up to 2-digit dividend) to solve problems.*

SOLVING PROBLEMS USING STRATEGIES FOR DIVISION

There are several strategies you can use to help you solve division problems. The following strategies may be useful to you. Remember, a personal strategy is a strategy that works best for you.

USING CONCRETE MATERIALS

You can use concrete materials like base ten blocks or counters to help you divide.

Example

Shawn picked 57 apples off the apple tree in his backyard. He wants to divide them into 5 equal groups. The following example shows how Shawn can use base ten blocks to show 57 ÷ 5 to find how many apples will belong to each group.

The number 57 has 5 tens and 7 ones, so it can be represented with 5 ten rods and 7 units.

Divide the blocks into 5 equal groups by placing 1 ten rod and 1 unit in each group.
1 ten rod + 1 unit = 11

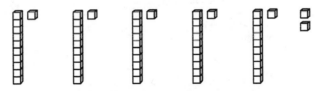

Shawn can make 5 equal groups with 11 apples in each group. He will have 2 apples left over.
57 ÷ 5 = 11 R2

USING ARRAYS

You can use an array to help you divide. Use the following steps to divide using an array:

1. Draw the same picture or symbol in columns or rows to make a rectangular shape.
2. Draw a circle around the number you want in each group—the number you are dividing by.
3. Count the number of groups you have. This is the answer to the division.

Example

Sherry had 42 stickers. She gave 7 stickers each to some friends. How many friends received stickers from Sherry?

To find how many friends each got 7 stickers, you need to divide.
42 ÷ 7 = ?

Use an array like the one shown to help you divide 42 by 7.

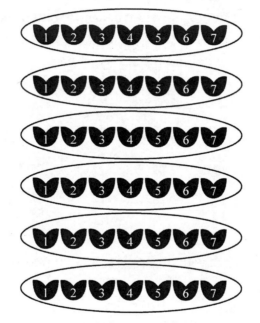

42 ÷ 7 = 6

Sherry gave 7 stickers each to 6 friends.

USING NUMBERS (SYMBOLIC REPRESENTATIONS)

You can use a standard algorithm to solve a division problem. An algorithm is a set of steps that you follow when you calculate.

:Example

Maya has 37 paperclips. She uses them to make squares. She uses 4 paperclips to make each square.

To find how many squares Maya can make out of 37 paperclips, you need to divide.
$37 \div 4 = \square$

Step 1

Write the total number (dividend) inside the division bracket (37).

Write the number you are dividing by the (divisor) in front of the bracket (4).
$$4\overline{)37}$$

Step 2

Use skip counting to determine how many groups of 4 there are in 37.
4, 8, 12, 16, 20, 24, 28, 32, 36→9 groups of 4

Place the 9 above the bracket over the 7 or 37.
$$\begin{array}{r} 9 \\ 4\overline{)37} \end{array}$$

Step 3

Since 4 × 9 = 36, write 36 below 37. Draw a line under the 36. Subtract the two numbers.
$$\begin{array}{r} 9 \\ 4\overline{)37} \\ \underline{36} \\ 1 \end{array}$$
$37 \div 4 = 9\,R1$

Sherry can make 9 squares. She will have 1 paperclip left over.

ESTIMATING QUOTIENTS

When you do not need an exact answer or you want to estimate an answer to get an idea of what the answer should be, you can estimate. You should use whatever estimation strategy works best for you. Two common strategies are front-end estimation and rounding.

Example

Sarah needs to solve this problem.
$96 \div 4 = ?$

She wants an estimate to show her "about" what the answer will be.

To solve this problem, Sarah can estimate the dividend by rounding 96 to the nearest hundred.
$96 \rightarrow 100$

Sarah knows that there are four groups of 25 in 100 (25, 50, 75, 100), so she does not change the 4.
$100 \div 4 = 25$

When Sarah does the actual calculation, she finds that
$96 \div 4 = 24$

She knows that she made a good estimate because the answer is very close to the estimate.

RELATING DIVISION TO MULTIPLICATION

Since division is the inverse or opposite operation of multiplication, you can use multiplication facts to help you solve division problems.

Example

You are asked to solve this division question.
$18 \div 3 = \square$

Think multiplication: What number times 3 equals 18?
$6 \times 3 = 18$ and $3 \times 6 = 18$

That means that $18 \div 3 = 6$ and $18 \div 6 = 3$.

Use the following information to answer the next question.

Jason sorts these 66 items into equal-sized groups.

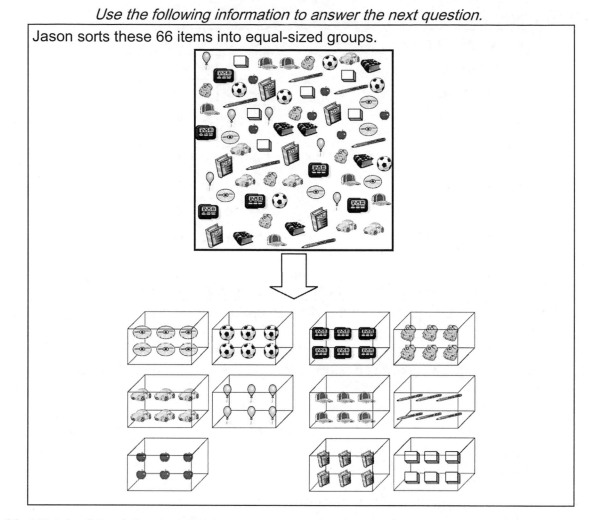

29. Which of the following division sentences represents the groups Jason made?

    A. $66 \div 2 = k$ **B.** $66 \div 4 = k$

    C. $66 \div 6 = k$ **D.** $66 \div 8 = k$

30. Which related multiplication fact could help solve the given division problem, $72 \div 8 = m$?

    A. $4 \times m = 72$ **B.** $6 \times m = 72$

    C. $72 = m \times 2$ **D.** $72 = m \times 8$

31. The array that represents $16 \div 4 = t$ is

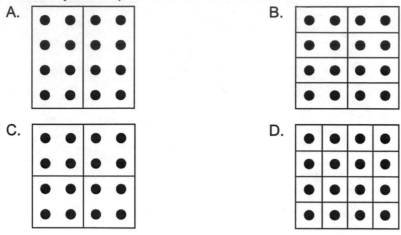

A.

B.

C.

D.

Use the following information to answer the next question.

Zara estimates the quotient for this division problem:
$43 \div 5 = w$

32. Which of the following division sentences would be **best** for Zara to use for her estimate?

A. $20 \div 5 = w$ B. $35 \div 5 = w$

C. $40 \div 5 = w$ D. $50 \div 5 = w$

Written Response

33. Write a word problem that can be solved by dividing 80 by 7.
$80 \div 7 = \square$

Explain how you solved the problem you wrote.

4N1.8 *Demonstrate an understanding of fractions less than or equal to one by using concrete, pictorial and symbolic representations.*

FRACTIONS LESS THAN OR EQUAL TO 1

Fractions are part of everyday life, so it is important to understand what fractions mean and how they work.

Fractions can be used when telling time. For example, lunch is in $\frac{1}{2}$ hour.

Fractions can be used when baking. For example, add $\frac{1}{4}$ cup of raisins to a cookie recipe.

Fractions can be used when dividing things evenly. For example, each person will eat $\frac{1}{3}$ of a pizza.

NAMING AND RECORDING FRACTIONS

Fractions are used to measure parts of a whole or parts of a set.

Parts of a Whole	Parts of a Set
	○ ○ ● ● ○ ○ ○ ○

There are two parts to a fraction: the numerator and the denominator.

The **denominator** is the number below the line. It represents the total number of parts in a whole or a set.

The **numerator** is the number above the line. It represents the number of parts that you are identifying or considering.

$\frac{3}{4}$ — numerator
— denominator

For example, the diagram above shows 4 equal parts of a whole, and 3 of the parts are white. The white parts of the diagram are represented by the fraction $\frac{3}{4}$ (three-quarters).

Fractions are named by their denominators. The following chart shows examples of the relationship between the denominator and the fractional name.

Denominator	Example Fraction	Fractional name
2 (equal parts)	$\frac{1}{2}$	One-half
3 (equal parts)	$\frac{2}{3}$	Two-thirds
5 (equal parts)	$\frac{3}{5}$	Three-fifths

COMPARING AND ORDERING FRACTIONS

SAME DENOMINATORS

You can compare and order fractions that have the same denominators (same bottom number). To compare the fractions, look at the numerators (top numbers).

- The smaller the number, the smaller the fraction.
- The greater the number, the greater the fraction.

Example

The diagrams below show a whole and a set divided into thirds.

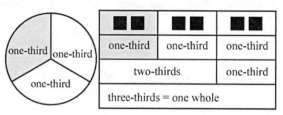

One-third represents $\frac{1}{3}$, two-thirds represents $\frac{2}{3}$, and three-thirds represents $\frac{3}{3}$.

From least to greatest, the order of the fractions is $\frac{1}{3}, \frac{2}{3}, \frac{3}{3}$.

SAME NUMERATORS

You can compare and order fractions that have the same numerators (same top number). To compare the fractions, look at the denominators (bottom numbers).

- The smaller the number, the greater the fraction.
- The greater the number, the smaller the fraction.

Example

Order the following fractions from least to greatest: $\dfrac{1}{5}, \dfrac{1}{2}, \dfrac{1}{4}, \dfrac{1}{10}$

To solve this problem, remember that the smaller the denominator, the greater the fraction.

That means that you need to order the denominators from the greatest number to the least number

Least fraction → $\dfrac{1}{10}, \dfrac{1}{5}, \dfrac{1}{4}, \dfrac{1}{2}$ ← Greatest fraction

Greatest number?   ? Least number

From least to greatest, the order of the fractions is $\dfrac{1}{10}, \dfrac{1}{5}, \dfrac{1}{4}, \dfrac{1}{2}$.

USING NUMBER LINES

You can compare and order fractions using **number lines**. For example, the following number line shows the benchmarks of 0 and 1. The space between the benchmarks is divided into tenths.

You can show the order of the fractions $\dfrac{5}{10}, \dfrac{3}{10}$, and $\dfrac{10}{10}$ on the number line by starting at the zero and counting the number of tenths in each fraction.

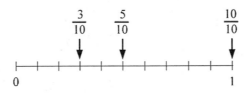

SAME FRACTIONS, DIFFERENT QUANTITIES

When you compare fractions, the fractions must represent the same size whole.
Two identical fractions may not represent the same quantity for different wholes.

:Example

Jenna and Ashley went to a restaurant, and they each ordered a pizza. Jenna ordered a small pizza and Ashley ordered a large pizza. Each girl ate one-half of her pizza.

Jenna's Pizza

Ashley's Pizza

The fraction $\frac{1}{2}$ represents the amount that each girl ate.

However, when you compare the size of each girl's half, Ashley's half is much greater in size than Jenna's half.

Jenna's half: 1/2

Ashley's half: 1/2

---

34. There were 5 apples in Mya's fridge.

    If Mya ate 2 of the apples, then what fraction of the apples were **not** eaten?

    A. $\frac{2}{5}$ B. $\frac{1}{2}$ C. $\frac{3}{5}$ D. $\frac{2}{3}$

35. Which of the following fractions is **greater** than $\frac{5}{8}$?

    A. $\frac{1}{8}$ B. $\frac{2}{8}$ C. $\frac{4}{8}$ D. $\frac{7}{8}$

36. Which of the following sets of fractions are ordered from least to greatest?

A. $\frac{3}{5}, \frac{2}{5}, \frac{4}{5}$ B. $\frac{3}{4}, \frac{2}{4}, \frac{1}{4}$

C. $\frac{1}{3}, \frac{3}{3}, \frac{2}{3}$ D. $\frac{1}{5}, \frac{2}{5}, \frac{5}{5}$

37. The fraction $\frac{3}{4}$ is represented by the dot on which of the following number lines?

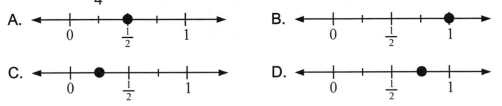

A.   B.

C.   D.

<u>**Written Response**</u>

38. Represent the fraction $\frac{2}{5}$ by shading in parts of the circle.

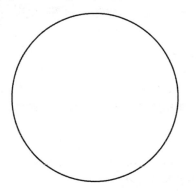

<u>**Written Response**</u>

39. Order these fractions by placing them on the given number line, using the given benchmarks of 0 and 1.

$\frac{9}{10}, \frac{1}{10}, \frac{5}{10}$

0   1

4N1.9 *Represent and describe decimals (tenths and hundredths), concretely, pictorially and symbolically.*

DESCRIBING AND REPRESENTING DECIMALS

Like fractions, decimals are used to represent parts of a whole or set. Decimals can show tenths (ten equal parts) or hundredths (one hundred equal parts).

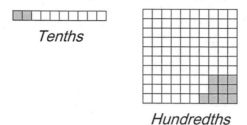

Tenths

Hundredths

The following place value chart shows the relationship between whole numbers and decimal numbers. The first number to the left of the decimal point is the ones place value. It is a whole number. The numbers to the right of the decimal point show the parts of a whole or parts of a set.

Ones	Decimal	Tenths	Hundredths
	●		

The first number to the right of the decimal point is the **tenths** place value, and the second number to the right of the decimal point is the **hundredths** place value.

TENTHS

If a whole has ten equal parts, like a ten rod, the decimal will be in tenths. For example, there are 6 units shaded on this ten rod.

The decimal that represents the number of shaded units is 0.6. The 0 tells you that the number is less than one whole. The 6 tells you that six out of ten parts are shaded.

Ones	Decimal	Tenths	Hundredths
0	●	6	

Example

☀ ☀ ☀ ☀ ☀ ☀ ☀ ☀ ☀ ☀

What decimal number represents the number of shaded suns in the set of suns?

The decimal that represents the number of shaded suns is 0.5.
The 0 tells you that the whole set is not shaded. There is no whole number.
The 5 tells you that 5 of the 10 suns are shaded.

HUNDREDTHS

If a whole has one hundred equal parts, like a hundred flat, the decimal will be in hundredths. For example, there are 45 units shaded on this hundred flat.

The decimal that represents the number of shaded units is 0.45. The 0 tells you that the number is less than one whole. The 45 tells you that 45 of the 100 parts are shaded.

Ones	Decimal	Tenths	Hundredths
0	●	4	5

EQUIVALENT DECIMALS

Decimal numbers that are **equivalent** have the same value when you compare them.

For example, 0.4 (four-tenths) has the same value as 0.40 (forty-hundredths).
0.4 = 0.40

Adding a 0 after the last digit of a decimal number does not change the value.

Think of money to help you understand equivalent decimals.

For example, 0.7 and 0.70 are equivalent in the same way that 7 dimes and 70 pennies are equivalent. They both have a value of seventy cents.

DECIMALS IN MONEY

There are 100 cents in one dollar, so all cent values from 1 cent to 99 cents are written in the hundredths.

- Writing cent values from 1 cent to 9 cents:
  Write a 0 in the tenths place to make sure the tenths position is open.
  For example, 3 cents out of 100 cents is written as $0.03.
- Writing cent values that end in 10:
  Write a 0 to keep the hundredths position open. For example, 30 cents out of 100 cents is written as $0.30.

Use the following information to answer the next question.

The given circle is divided into ten equal parts with some of the parts shaded and some of the parts not shaded.

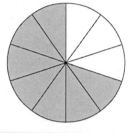

40. The shaded part of the circle can be represented by the decimal number

A. 0.07   B. 0.7

C. 3.7   D. 7.0

Use the following information to answer the next question.

Jake shades squares on a hundredths chart to represent a decimal number.

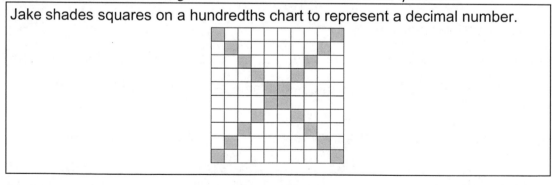

41. The decimal number that is represented by the shaded squares on the hundredths chart is

A. 0.02   B. 0.20

C. 0.22   D. 2.00

42. In which of the following hundredths charts does the shaded part represent the decimal 0.12?

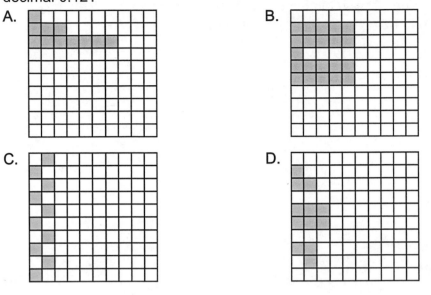

A.

B.

C.

D.

43. Which of the following sets of coins represents the decimal number 0.43?

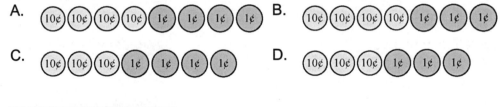

A. (10¢)(10¢)(10¢)(10¢)(1¢)(1¢)(1¢)(1¢)   B. (10¢)(10¢)(10¢)(10¢)(1¢)(1¢)(1¢)

C. (10¢)(10¢)(10¢)(1¢)(1¢)(1¢)(1¢)   D. (10¢)(10¢)(10¢)(1¢)(1¢)(1¢)

Numerical Response

44. In the number 57.03, which digit is in the tenths place? _____

45. Explain the meaning of each digit in the decimal number 55.55. You may use a chart or diagram to help you explain your answer.

4N1.10 *Relate decimals to fractions and fractions to decimals (to hundredths).*

RELATING DECIMALS TO FRACTIONS

Just like decimals can be equivalent to each other (0.4 and 0.40), decimals and fractions can also be equivalent to each other.

Example

The given figure shows 4 squares shaded out of a total of 10 squares.

The fraction that represents the shaded part of the figure is $\frac{4}{10}$. The decimal that represents the shaded part of the figure is 0.4.

The decimal 0.4 is equivalent to $\frac{4}{10}$.

$0.4 = \frac{4}{10}$

In this figure, 40 squares are shaded out of a total of 100 squares.

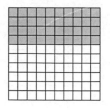

The fraction that represents the shaded part of the figure is $\frac{40}{100}$. The decimal that represents the shaded part of the figure is 0.40.

The decimal 0.40 is equivalent to $\frac{40}{100}$.

$$0.40 = \frac{40}{100}$$

READING DECIMALS AS FRACTIONS

When you read decimals as fractions, you start with the word *zero*, say the word *and* where the decimal point is, and then use fractional names for the decimal part of the number. Do not say the word *decimal*.

For example, to read 0.4 as a fraction, say "zero and four tenths". To read 0.15 as a fraction, say "zero and fifteen hundredths".

Use the following information to answer the next question.

The shaded part of the given grid can be represented by an equivalent decimal and fraction.

46. Which of the following decimal and fraction sets can represent the shaded part of the given grid?

   A. 0.4 and $\frac{4}{10}$ B. 0.40 and $\frac{40}{100}$

   C. 0.36 and $\frac{36}{10}$ D. 0.36 and $\frac{36}{100}$

47. Josh ate $\frac{3}{10}$ of a chocolate bar. The decimal that represents how much he ate is

   A. 0.3   B. 3.0

   C. 3.10   D. 10.3

Use the following information to answer the next question.

The fraction $\frac{9}{10}$ represents the shaded part of the given figure.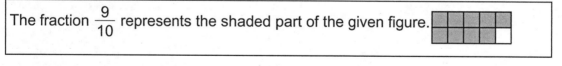

Numerical Response

48. What equivalent decimal represents the shaded part of the given figure? _____

4N1.11 *Demonstrate an understanding of addition and subtraction of decimals (limited to hundredths).*

ADDING AND SUBTRACTING DECIMALS

When adding or subtracting decimal numbers, it is important to line up the decimal points. The actual adding and subtracting of decimals is like adding and subtracting whole numbers. Start at the right and work toward the left, regrouping when necessary. Remember to put the decimal point in the proper place in your answer.

If the numbers you are adding or subtracting do not have the same number of digits in the tenths and hundredths places, you can put a zero after the tenths numbers. This will not change the value of the numbers. It might make it easier to keep the numbers in line.

Example

To add 1.12 + 3.2 + 4.32, you can write the numbers in columns as shown.

Example 1 shows 3.2 written without a zero added after the two-tenths.

Example 2 shows 3.2 written with a zero added after the two-tenths (3.20).

Example 1	Example 2
1.12	1.12
3.2←	3.20←
4.32	4.32
8.64	8.64

ESTIMATING SUMS AND DIFFERENCES

There are several strategies for estimating sums or differences when adding or subtracting decimals. Following are two examples: rounding the decimal numbers to the nearest whole numbers and using front-end estimation.

ROUNDING TO THE NEAREST WHOLE NUMBER

You can round the decimals to the nearest whole number and then add or subtract the estimated numbers. You can use a number line to help you see which whole numbers are closest to the decimal numbers.

Example

Ryder wants to estimate the sum of 5.75 + 8.12. He uses a number line that starts with 5 (whole number before 5.75) and ends with 9 (whole number after 8.12).

He then places the two decimal numbers on the number line.

The decimal 5.75 is between 5 and 6, but is closest to 6.

The decimal 8.12 is between 8 and 9, but is closest to 8.

Ryder then adds the two estimated numbers (addends).
6 + 8 = 14

The estimated sum of 5.75 + 8.12 is 14.

USING FRONT-END ESTIMATION

You can use the first digit (greatest place value) of the numbers, turning the rest of the digits into zeros. You can then add or subtract the estimated numbers. Remember that front-end estimation always gives a lower "about" answer when adding.

Example

Gary has $74.25. He buys some clothes that cost $42.89.
About how much money will Gary get back in change?

Step 1
Using front-end estimation to round the numbers.
$74.25 → $70.00
$42.89 → $40.00

Step 2
Subtract.
$70.00 – $40.00 = $30.00
Gary will get about $30.00 back in change.

Using Mental Strategies

Mental strategies are plans that help you add or subtract decimals in your head. This usually means breaking numbers into easier forms to work with. Following are examples of strategies that may help you.

Round the decimal numbers to make whole numbers ending in 0. Add the estimated numbers. From the sum, subtract the total value of the digits you added to make the whole numbers.

:Example

Franco bought two plants. One plant cost $12.99 and the other plant cost $10.89. What is the total cost of both plants?

To find the total cost of the plants, you need to add.
$12.99 + $10.89 = □
This is a quick way to add $12.99 + $10.89 = $23.88.

Step 1
Round the decimal numbers to make whole numbers.
Add 1 cent to $12.99 to make $13.00.
Add 11 cents to $10.89 to make $11.00.

Step 2
Add the estimated numbers.
$13.00 + $11.00 = $24.00

Step 3
Subtract the 12 cents that you added (1¢ plus 11¢).
$24.00 – $0.12 = $23.88

A strategy that works well when determining the amount of change you should get when you make a purchase is to count up from the purchase price to the amount you paid with.

:Example

Max bought a kite for $14.98. He paid with a twenty dollar bill.
How much change should Max get back?

Step 1
Round the decimal numbers to whole numbers.
Count up from $14.98 to the nearest dollar. Two cents will take you to $15.00.
Count up from $15.00 to $20.00. Five dollars will take you from $15.00 to $20.00

Step 2
Add the two amounts.
$0.02 + $5.00 = $5.02
Max should get $5.02 back in change.

Use the following information to answer the next question.

When Lee's mom cleaned out her purse, she gave Lee $11.03.
When Lee's dad cleaned out his pockets, he gave Lee $6.87.

49. Which of the following estimates **best** shows about how much money Lee got from her mom and dad?
    A. $15.00   B. $16.00
    C. $18.00   D. $20.00

Use the following information to answer the next question.

Mr. and Mrs. Parker ordered a pizza that was cut into ten equal pieces.
Mr. Parker ate 0.5 of the pizza and Mrs. Parker ate 0.3 of the pizza.

50. The decimal that represents the amount of pizza that Mr. and Mrs. Parker did **not** eat is
    A. 1.2   B. 1.0   C. 0.8   D. 0.2

51. Jerry and his grandma went shopping for some new clothes. The cost of the new clothes was $47.37.

    How much money was left after Jerry's grandma paid for the clothes with three twenty dollar bills?

    A. $12.37   B. $12.63
    C. $12.72   D. $13.73

52. Fred is asked to find the sum of 10.25 + 8.75.

One strategy Fred can use to find the sum is

A. 10 + 8

B. 11 + 9

C. 10 + 8 + 1

D. 10 + 9 + 1

ANSWERS AND SOLUTIONS
NUMBER

1. C	12. 9250	23. 9	34. C	45. WR
2. C	13. A	24. C	35. D	46. D
3. D	14. C	25. D	36. D	47. A
4. B	15. A	26. A	37. D	48. 0.9
5. A	16. C	27. D	38. WR	49. C
6. WR	17. C	28. 384	39. WR	50. D
7. WR	18. 1200	29. C	40. B	51. B
8. C	19. 80	30. D	41. B	52. C
9. B	20. WR	31. C	42. D	
10. C	21. B	32. C	43. B	
11. A	22. C	33. WR	44. 0	

1. C

The numeral 5 243 represents the expanded notation 5 000 + 200 + 40 + 3.

The numeral and the expanded notation both show 5 thousands, 2 hundreds, 4 tens, and 3 ones.

2. C

The expanded notation form of 3 042 is 3 000 + 40 + 2.

In the numeral 3 042, there are 3 thousands, 0 hundreds, 4 tens, and 2 ones.

3. D

In the number 1 005, the value of the digit 1 is 1 000.

In the number 1 005, there is 1 thousand and 5 ones. There are no hundreds and no tens.

4. B

The place value chart that represents the number 7 113 is as follows:

Thousands	Hundreds	Tens	Ones
7	1	1	3

In the number 7 113, there are 7 thousands, 1 hundred, 1 ten, and 3 ones.

5. A

The digit 8 is in the thousands place, so it has a value of 8 000.

Thousands	Hundreds	Tens	Ones
8	9	6	7

6. WR

The numeral 3 534 can be represented in written form as "three thousand five hundred thirty-four."

Remember the following points:

- Do not use the word *and* after the thousands or hundreds.
- Use a hyphen between the tens and the ones for numbers between 21 and 99 that do not end in a zero.

7. WR

Example Explanation
In the number 9 872,

- The digit 9 means that there are 9 thousands: 9 000
- The digit 8 means that there are 8 hundreds: 800
- The digit 7 means that there are 7 tens: 70
- The digit 2 means that there are 2 ones: 2

Place Value Chart

Thousands	Hundreds	Tens	Ones
9	8	7	2

8. C

The set of numbers that is in ascending order is 8 175, 8 200, 8 478.

Remember: Ascending order is from least value to greatest value.

Since there are 8 thousands in each number, you need to compare the hundreds.

Since 1 < 2 and 2 < 4, then
8 175 < 8 200 and 8 200 < 8 478

9. B

This number line shows the arrow that could represent the number 710:

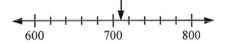

The ticks on the number line count up by 20s.

That means that the first tick after 700 represents the number 720.

The space halfway between 700 and the first tick represents the number 710.

10. C

Janelle placed a number incorrectly in this set of numbers: 908, 1 118, 1 108, 1 308.

The number 1 118 should be placed after 1 108: 908, 1 108, 1 118, 1 308.

11. A

The number Lois placed incorrectly is 3 050.

Lois placed 3 050 on the tick that represents 3 500. It should have been placed halfway between the number 3 000 and the first tick, which represents the number 3 100.

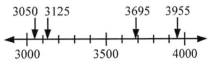

12. 9250

Each tick on the number line represents 250: (8 000, 8 250, 8 500, 8 750, 9 000)

The first tick after the number 9 000 represents the number 9 250.

13. A

The mountain in Tibet is 1 658 m higher than the mountain in Tanzania.

To find the difference in heights, you need to subtract the height of the mountain in Tanzania from the height of the mountain in Tibet.
7 553 − 5 895 = 1 658

14. C

The expanded notation of
1 000 + 300 + 30 + 1 represents the solution to Jacob's problem.

Example strategy
2 651 = 2 000 + 600 + 50 + 1
1 320 = 1 000 + 300 + 20 + 1

$$\begin{array}{r} 2\ 000 + 600 + 50 + 1 \\ -\ 1\ 000 + 300 + 20 + 0 \\ \hline 1\ 000 + 300 + 30 + 1 \end{array}$$

15. A

You can estimate the number of apples needed to bake ten pies because apples vary in size. All the other choices need exact answers.

16. C

At the end of 6 months, Conner will have a total of 5 162 cards.

To determine the number of cards Conner will receive from the club, count by 100 for 6 counts.
(100, 200, 300, 400, 500, 600) or multiply 6 by 100:
6 × 100 = 600

Add the amount he has right now to the amount he gets from the club.
4 562 + 600 = 5 162

17. C

The **best** estimate for the sum of 535 and 207 is 700.

Example Strategy:
Using front-end estimation, 535 → 500 and 207 → 200.
500 + 200 = 700

18. 1200

Pam, Jon, and Mario used about 1 200 sunflower seeds altogether.

When you use front-end estimation, you only use the digit in the greatest place value. All the numbers to the right of that digit are replaced by zeros.
384 → 300
422 → 400
516 → 500
300 + 400 + 500 = 1 200

19. 80

When you multiply a number by 1, the answer will always be the number itself.

20. WR

49 ÷ 1 = 49

Example explanation
When you apply the property of 1 for division, that means that when you divide any number by 1, the answer will always be that number.

21. B

She started with a double (2 × 8) and then added another group of 8.

That means that she had 3 groups of 8, which is 3 × 8.

The math fact Trish was solving was 3 × 8 = K.

22. C

The related multiplication fact that will help Raj is 9 × 7 = m.

Since 9 × 7 = 63, then 63 ÷ 9 = 7.

23. 9

Kent was multiplying by 9.

The known fact that Kent started from was 2 × 9 = 18.

He then skip counted by 9s until he got to 63, which was the answer to 7 × 9.
3 × 9 = 27
4 × 9 = 36
5 × 9 = 45
6 × 9 = 54
7 × 9 = 63

24. C

Ali and Miyu used a total of about 800 straws.

Example estimation
The number 212 is closer to 200 than to 300, so about 200 straws were used to build each bridge.

Since there were 4 bridges built, multiply the estimated number of straws by 4.
200 × 4 = 800

25. D

One strategy you can use to solve 3 × 110 is to apply the distributive property:
(3 × 100) + (3 × 10)
    110 = 100 + 10
3 × 110 = (3 × 100) + (3 × 10)
3 × 110 = 300 + 30
    330 = 330

26. A

There are 32 seats in each car.
2 × 16 = 32

A total of 64 passengers will fit in one car.
2 × 32 = 64

A total of 320 passengers will fit in 5 cars.
5 × 64 = 320

The greatest number of passengers the train can carry is 320.

27. D

The given array can be represented by this multiplication fact:
7 × 14 = 98

There are 7 rows of squares with 14 squares in every row.
14 = 10 + 4
(7 × 10) + (7 × 4)
70 + 28 = 98

28. 384

Liza would need 384 stickers to fill all three books.

Multiply 16 by 8 to find the number of stickers needed to fill one book:
16 × 8 = 128

Multiply 128 by 3 to find the number of stickers needed to fill three books:
128 × 3 = 384

29. C

The division sentence of 66 ÷ 6 = *k* represents the groups Jason made.

Jason sorted the 66 items by putting 6 of each similar item into a group. He made 11 groups.
66 ÷ 6 = 11

30. D

The related multiplication fact of
72 = *m* × 8 could help solve the division problem.

These are the four related facts that make up the fact family:
72 ÷ 8 = 9 and 72 ÷ 9 = 8
8 × 9 = 72 and 9 × 8 = 72

31. C

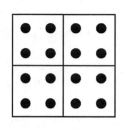

This array represents 16 ÷ 4 = *t*.

The array has a total of 16 dots, with 4 dots in each of the 4 groups. 16 ÷ 4 = 4

32. C

The division sentence that would be best for Zara to use is
40 ÷ 5 = *w*

Most estimates end in 0. Since 43 is closer to 40 than to 50,
43 → 40

Since all numbers that end in 0 are divisible by 5, the 5 does not need to change.
40 ÷ 5 = 8

33. WR

Example problem
Mrs. Barker has 80 new pencils. She asked Lana to put an equal number of pencils into each of the 7 pencil boxes. How many pencils should Lana put into each box? How many pencils will be left over?

Example explanation

- I knew that I needed to divide 80 by 7. This is how I divided.
- I knew that 7 × 11 = 77, so I knew that 80 divided by 7 was 11 with a remainder.
- I subtracted 77 from 80 to find the remainder:
  80 − 77 = 3

Lana needed to put 11 pencils in each pencil box. She had 3 pencils left over.

34. C

$\frac{3}{5}$ of the apples were **not** eaten.

Since there were 5 apples in all, the number 5 will be the denominator (bottom number) of the fraction.

Since Mya ate 2 apples, there are 3 apples left. That means that 3 will be the numerator (top number) of the fraction.

35. D

The fraction $\frac{7}{8}$ is greater than the fraction $\frac{5}{8}$.

Since the denominators are the same, compare the numerators.

Since 7 > 5, then $\frac{7}{8} > \frac{5}{8}$.

36. D

This set of fractions $\frac{1}{5}, \frac{2}{5}, \frac{5}{5}$, is ordered from least to greatest.

Since the denominators are the same, compare the numerators. The smaller the numerator, the smaller the fraction.

The number 1 is less than 2, and 2 is less than 5 or 1 < 2, and 2 < 5.

37. D

The fraction $\frac{3}{4}$ is represented by the dot on this number line.

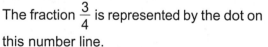

The fraction $\frac{3}{4}$ is greater than $\frac{1}{2}$ and less than the whole number 1.

38. WR

To represent the fraction $\frac{2}{5}$, the circle needs to be divided into 5 equal parts, with any 2 of the parts being shaded.

Example representation of $\frac{2}{5}$

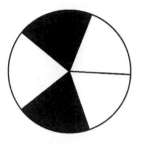

39. WR

Starting at the 0, $\frac{1}{10}$ is placed at the first tick.

$\frac{5}{10}$ is placed at the fifth or middle tick, which is the halfway mark on the given number line $\left(\frac{5}{10} = \frac{1}{2}\right)$.

$\frac{9}{10}$ is placed at the ninth or second last tick, just before the whole number.

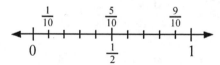

40. B

The shaded part of the circle can be represented by the decimal number 0.7.

Since there are ten parts to the circle, the decimal will be in the tenths place.
There are 7 parts that are shaded, so the decimal number is written as 0.7.

41. B

The decimal number that is represented by the 20 shaded squares on the hundredths chart is 0.20 (twenty-hundredths).

42. D

The shaded part of this hundredths chart represents the decimal 0.12.

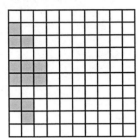

To represent the decimal 0.12, twelve of the hundred squares must be shaded.

43. B

This set of coins represents the decimal number 0.43.

The decimal 0.43 represents 43 hundredths, which is the same as 43 cents out of one dollar.
The 4 in the tenths position is represented by 4 dimes.
The 3 in the hundredths position is represented by 3 pennies.

44. 0

In the number 57.03, the digit 0 is in the tenths place.

Tens	Ones	.	Tenths	Hundredths
5	7	.	0	3

45. WR

Example explanation
Starting at the left, the first 5 represents 5 tens: 50.
The next 5 represents 5 ones: 5.
The first 5 to the right of the decimal point represents 5 tenths: 0.5 or $\frac{5}{10}$.
The second 5 to the right of the decimal point represents 5 hundredths: 0.05 or $\frac{5}{100}$.

Tens	Ones	.	Tenths	Hundredths
5	5	.	5	5

46. D

Since 36 of the 100 squares are shaded, the decimal and fraction set that represents the shaded part of the given grid is 0.36 and $\frac{36}{100}$.

47. A

The decimal 0.3 represents how much chocolate Josh ate.

Josh ate 3 out of 10 pieces of chocolate. The decimal 0.3 is equivalent to the fraction $\frac{3}{10}$.

48. 0.9

The equivalent decimal to $\frac{9}{10}$ is 0.9.

The figure has ten equal parts with nine of the parts shaded, so the fraction and equivalent decimal are in the tenths.

49. C

The estimate of $18.00 best shows the amount of money Lee got from her mom and dad.

Example strategy
Round each money value to the nearest dollar.

- $11.03 is closest to $11.00.
- $6.87 is closest to $7.00.

Add the two estimates together:
$11.00 + $7.00 = $18.00.

50. **D**

The decimal 0.2 represents the amount of pizza that Mr. and Mrs. Parker did not eat.

The decimal that represents the whole pizza is 1.0.

The decimal 0.8 represents the pizza that Mr. and Mrs. Parker ate.
0.5 + 0.3 = 0.8

To find which decimal represents the amount not eaten, subtract 0.8 from 1.0.
1.0 – 0.8 = 0.2

51. **B**

Jerry's grandma had $12.63 left after she paid for the clothes.

Three twenty dollar bills is equal to $60.00.
$60.00 – $47.37 = $12.63

52. **C**

One strategy Fred can use to solve the problem is 10 + 8 + 1.

Example strategy

- First add the whole numbers.
  10 + 8 = 18
- Then, add the decimal numbers.
  0.25 + 0.75 = 1.00
  (Think of how adding 1 quarter and 3 quarters makes 1 dollar.)
- Add the extra whole number to the whole number 18.
  18 + 1 = 19
- 10.25 + 8.75 = 19.0

UNIT TEST

1. The numeral that represents the expanded notation form of 9 000 + 500 + 60 is

   A. 956   B. 9 056

   C. 9 506   D. 9 560

2. The numeral 8 603 expressed in expanded notation is

   A. 800 + 60 + 3   B. 8 000 + 60 + 3

   C. 8 000 + 600 + 3   D. 8 000 + 600 + 30

3. In the number 9 876, the digit 7 represents 7

   A. thousands   B. hundreds

   C. tens   D. ones

4. Which of the following place value charts represents the number 1 101?

   A.
Thousands	Hundreds	Tens	Ones
1	1	1	1

   B.
Thousands	Hundreds	Tens	Ones
1	1	10	1

   C.
Thousands	Hundreds	Tens	Ones
1	10	0	1

   D.
Thousands	Hundreds	Tens	Ones
1	1	0	1

Numerical Response

5. What numeral does the expanded notation 6 000 + 20 + 8 represent? _____

6. The distance between two cities is about 3 333 kilometres.

    Explain the meaning of each digit in the number 3 333. You may use a chart or diagram to help you explain your answer.

Written Response

7. How is the numeral 1 405 represented in written words?

8. Which of the following sets of numbers is written in descending order?
    A. 3 790, 9 370, 7 930   B. 9 370, 7 930, 3 790
    C. 3 790, 7 930, 9 370   D. 9 370, 3 790, 7 930

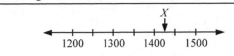

9. Which of the following numbers does the letter *X* represent on the given number line?

   A. 1 405   B. 1 425

   C. 1 450   D. 1 475

10. Kujo wrote the following set of numbers in descending order:
    9 009, 9 900, 9 099, 9 090

    The number that Kujo placed **incorrectly** is

    A. 9 009   B. 9 090

    C. 9 099   D. 9 900

   Written Response

11. Using the digits 7, 4, 9, 2, create and order three different 4-digit numerals.

    Label the order of numerals you created as ascending or descending.

Use the following information to answer the next question.

One weekend, a book store placed 1 052 books on sale. On Saturday, 401 books were sold. On Sunday, 542 books were sold.

12. How many of the books on sale were **not** sold on Saturday or Sunday?

    A. 108   B. 109

    C. 111   D. 119

13. In which of the following situations would an estimate rather than an exact answer be sufficient?
    A. Buying grapes to eat at lunchtime
    B. Making treats for each student in the class
    C. Measuring cups of flour when baking bread
    D. Counting the kinds of beads needed to make a necklace

Use the following information to answer the next question.

Quin has 3 647 stickers in her sticker collection. She buys 260 more stickers at a garage sale. On the way home, she loses 15 of the stickers.

14. How many stickers does Quin now have in her collection?
    A. 3 992   B. 3 912
    C. 3 907   D. 3 892

Use the following information to answer the next question.

Yoshi estimates the difference between 6 310 and 2 129.

15. Which of the following numbers is the **best** estimate of the difference between 6 310 and 2 129?
    A. 3 000   B. 4 000
    C. 5 000   D. 8 000

Use the following information to answer the next question.

When Enzo cleaned up the science corner in his classroom, he counted 214 straws in one box, 461 straws in another box, and 187 straws in a third box.

16. Using the estimation strategy of compensation, about how many straws were there in total?
    A. 700   B. 800
    C. 900   D. 1 000

Use the following information to answer the next question.

Brad and Norm collect hockey cards. Brad has 1 384 cards. Norm has 1 937 cards.

Numerical Response

17. How many cards do the two boys have together? _____

18. Which of the following problems can be solved by 3 ÷ 1 = 3?
    A. Luis had 3 pencils. He gave the pencils to a friend. How many pencils does his friend have?

    B. Claude had 3 stickers. He gave 1 sticker to Sam. How many stickers does Claude now have?

    C. Pam had 3 erasers. She gave 1 eraser each to some friends. How many friends got an eraser?

    D. Mei had 3 rulers. Russ gave her 1 more ruler. How many rulers does Mei now have?

Use the following information to answer the next question.

Each student in a Grade Four class gets one carton of milk for lunch. There are 22 students in the class.
Britt writes the following equation to determine the number of cartons used by all 22 students for one lunch.
$1 \times 22 = \square$

Written Response

19. Determine the answer to Britt's equation by explaining the property of 1 for multiplication.

20. One strategy Leela can use to find the answer to $9 \times 7 = K$ is to multiply 7 by 10 and then
    A. add 7   B. subtract 7

    C. divide by 7   D. multiply by 7

Use the following information to answer the next question.

Each morning, Bill's teacher writes some math facts on the board for the students to solve.
The fact Bill must solve is 72 ÷ 8 = *Z*.

21. Which of the following related multiplication facts should Bill use to help him solve
72 ÷ 8 = *Z*?
   A. 7 × 8 = □   B. 8 × 8 = □
   C. 8 × 9 = □   D. 10 × 8 = □

Use the following information to answer the next question.

Baskets and bags of corn on the cob are for sale at the farmers' market.
Each basket has 23 cobs of corn. Each bag has 2 times as many cobs of corn
as there are in one basket. Lucas's dad bought 6 bags of corn on the cob.

22. Which is the **best** estimate of how many cobs of corn Lucas's dad bought?
   A. 50   B. 150
   C. 200   D. 300

23. Which of the following mathematical statements is **true**?
   A. 7 × 105 = (7 × 10) + (7 × 5)   B. 7 × 105 = (7 × 100) + (7 × 5)
   C. 7 × 105 = (7 × 100) + (7 × 15)   D. 7 × 105 = (7 × 1) + (7 × 0)+(7 × 5)

24. What is the product when 508 is multiplied by 2?
   A. 1 006   B. 1 016
   C. 1 106   D. 1 116

Use the following information to answer the next question.

The zookeepers moved 12 elephants from their yard to a larger yard.
The zookeepers placed three elephants in each row and moved the elephants as one group.

25. Which of the following arrays shows how the elephants were grouped for the move?

A.

B.

C.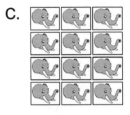

D.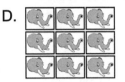

26. Roxie uses the strategy of skip counting backward to show her understanding of division.

Which of the following sets of numbers shows the skip counting pattern that could help Roxie divide by 8?

A. 90, 82, 74, 66…

B. 81, 72, 63, 54…

C. 80, 72, 63, 56…

D. 72, 64, 56, 48…

Use the following information to answer the next question.

For a snack, 4 children equally shared a box of mini pretzels.

27. If there were 96 pretzels in the box, how many pretzels did each child get?

A. 26

B. 24

C. 22

D. 20

Use the following information to answer the next question.

Leon had 59 comic books that he no longer wanted to keep. He divided them evenly among 7 friends. He donated the remaining comics to the school library.

Numerical Response

28. How many comic books did Leon donate to the school library? _____

29. The shaded part of which of the following diagrams represents the fraction $\frac{9}{10}$?

A.

B.

C.

D.

30. Which of the following fractions is **less** than $\frac{3}{6}$?

A. $\frac{1}{6}$

B. $\frac{3}{6}$

C. $\frac{4}{6}$

D. $\frac{6}{6}$

31. Which of the following sets of fractions is ordered from greatest to least?

A. $\frac{4}{10}, \frac{6}{10}, \frac{10}{10}$

B. $\frac{9}{10}, \frac{6}{10}, \frac{5}{10}$

C. $\frac{8}{10}, \frac{6}{10}, \frac{7}{10}$

D. $\frac{9}{10}, \frac{3}{10}, \frac{6}{10}$

32. Which of the following sets of fractions is ordered from least to greatest?

A. $\frac{1}{2}, \frac{1}{8}, \frac{1}{6}, \frac{1}{4}$

B. $\frac{1}{4}, \frac{1}{3}, \frac{1}{2}, \frac{1}{5}$

C. $\frac{1}{8}, \frac{1}{4}, \frac{1}{5}, \frac{1}{3}$

D. $\frac{1}{6}, \frac{1}{5}, \frac{1}{3}, \frac{1}{2}$

Use the following information to answer the next question.

Numerical Response

33. In the given set of pencils, what fraction represents the number of pencils that are circled? _____

Use the following information to answer the next question.

Shabir says that the fraction $\frac{1}{3}$ is **less** than the fraction $\frac{1}{5}$.

Tessa says that the fraction $\frac{1}{3}$ is **greater** than the fraction $\frac{1}{5}$.

Written Response

34. Who is correct?

Explain how denominators can be used to compare two given fractions with the numerator 1.

Use the following information to answer the next question.

Cara shades these squares on a hundredths chart to show a decimal number.

35. The decimal number that Cara showed on the hundredths chart is

    A. 0.04   B. 0.05

    C. 0.40   D. 0.50

36. The white parts of which of the following figures represent the decimal 0.6?

    A.   B.

    C.   D.

37. The set of coins that can be used to represent the decimal number 0.38 is

    A. 3 dimes and 8 pennies   B. 8 dimes and 3 pennies

    C. 3 nickels and 8 pennies   D. 8 nickels and 3 pennies

38. The decimal number that is related to the fraction $\dfrac{7}{100}$ is

    A. 0.07   B. 0.70

    C. 7.00   D. 70.0

Use the following information to answer the next question.

Chris colours squares on a hundredths grid.

39. What decimal represents the coloured squares Chris coloured?

    A. 0.02   **B.** 0.20

    C. 2.00   **D.** 20.0

Use the following information to answer the next question.

Su-ling bought two books. One book cost $6.98 and the other book cost $5.99.

40. Which of the following strategies can be used to find the combined cost of the two books Su-ling bought?

    A. $7.00 + $6.00   **B.** $6.00 + $5.00 + $2.00

    C. $7.00 + $6.00 + $0.03   **D.** $7.00 + $6.00 − $0.03

41. Which of the following problems has an estimated sum of 350?

    A. 309.8 + 31.9   **B.** 329.8 + 10.2

    C. 250.75 + 99.25   **D.** 210.85 + 110.75

Use the following information to answer the next question.

Brian washed cars for two days to earn money for the animal shelter. On Saturday he earned $161.83, and on Sunday he earned $88.90.

42. How much money did Brian earn for the animal shelter?

    A. $249.73   **B.** $250.00

    C. $250.73   **D.** $251.00

Use the following information to answer the next question.

Rosa bought 4.6 m of red ribbon for a project she was working on. She went back to the store the next day and bought 1.75 m of white ribbon for the same project.

Numerical Response

43. How much ribbon did Rosa buy in total? _____ m

ANSWERS AND SOLUTIONS – UNIT TEST

1. D	10. A	19. WR	28. 3	37. A
2. C	11. WR	20. B	29. B	38. A
3. C	12. B	21. C	30. A	39. B
4. D	13. A	22. D	31. B	40. D
5. 6028	14. D	23. B	32. D	41. C
6. WR	15. B	24. B	33.	42. C
7. WR	16. B	25. C	34. WR	43. 6.35
8. B	17. 3321	26. D	35. B	
9. B	18. C	27. B	36. C	

1. D

The numeral 9 560 represents the expanded notation form of 9 000 + 500 + 60.

In the numeral 9 560, there are 9 thousands, 5 hundreds, 6 tens, and 0 ones.

2. C

The numeral 8 603 expressed in expanded notation is 8 000 + 600 + 3.

In the numeral 8 603, there are 8 thousands, 6 hundreds, 0 tens, and 3 ones.

3. C

In the number 9 876, the digit 7 represents 7 tens.

Thousands	Hundreds	Tens	Ones
9	8	7	6

4. D

The place value chart that represents the number 1 101 is as follows:

Thousands	Hundreds	Tens	Ones
1	1	0	1

In the number 1 101, there is 1 thousand, 1 hundred, 0 tens, and 1 one.

5. 6028

There are no hundreds in the expanded notation, so when you write the numeral, you need to put a zero in the hundreds place.

6. WR

Example explanation
Starting at the left, the first 3 of 3 333 stands for 3 thousands, 3 000.

The second 3 in 3 333 stands for 3 hundreds, 300.

The third 3 in 3 333 stands for 3 tens, 30.

The fourth 3 in 3 333 stands for 3 ones, 3.

Thousands	Hundreds	Tens	Ones
3	3	3	3
3 000	300	30	3

7. WR

The numeral 1 405 is represented in written words as "one thousand four hundred five."

When representing numerals in written form, remember not to use the word *and* after the thousands or hundreds.

8. **B**

The set of numbers written in descending order is 9 370, 7 930, 3 790.

Descending order is from greatest value to least value.

The greatest value is 9 000. The next greatest value is 7 000. The least value is 3 000.

9. **B**

The letter X on the given number line represents the number 1 425.

- The numbers on the number line count by 100s.
  (1 200, 1 300, 1 400, 1 500)
- The ticks between each set of numbers represent numbers that end in 50s.
  (1 250, 1 350, 1 450)
- The space halfway between a number and the tick to the right of that number represents numbers that end in 25s.
  (1 225, 1 325, 1 425)

10. **A**

The number that Kujo placed incorrectly is 9 009.

The correct way to write these numbers in descending order is 9 900, 9 099, 9 090, 9 009.

11. **WR**

There are many different numerals that can be created using the four given digits.

The easiest sets to create are when each numeral begins with a different digit in the same position, such as 9 472 and 2 792.

The more challenging sets to create are when the digits are reversed, such as 4 792 and 4 972.

Example sets of numerals
Descending order (greatest to least):
9 472, 7 249, 4 972
Ascending order (least to greatest): 7 429, 9 427, 9 742

12. **B**

A total of 109 books that were on sale were not sold on Saturday or Sunday.

Example strategy
One way to solve this problem is to first add the number of books sold on Saturday and Sunday.
401 + 542 = 943

Next, subtract the number of books sold from the total number of books.
1 052 – 943 = 109

13. **A**

If you were buying grapes to eat at lunchtime, it would not be important to know exactly how many grapes were attached to each stem.

14. **D**

Quin now has 3 892 stickers in her collection.

Example strategy
Add the number of stickers Quin has to the number of stickers she bought at the garage sale.
3 647 + 260 = 3 907

Subtract the number of stickers she lost from the total number of stickers.
3 907 – 15 = 3 892

15. **B**

The best estimate of the difference is 4 000.

Remember: A difference is the answer to a question that uses subtraction.

Example strategy
Using front-end estimation,
6 310 → 6 000 and 2 129 → 2 000.

Subtract the two estimated numbers.
6 000 – 2 000 = 4 000

16. B

Using the estimation strategy of compensation, there were about 800 straws in total.

Compensation Strategy
214 → 200 (front number 2)
461 → 400 (front number 4)
187 → 200 (front number +1)
Add the three estimates together.
200 + 400 + 200 = 800

17. 3321

To solve this problem, add the two numbers together.
1 384 + 1937 = 3 321
The two boys have 3 321 cards together.

18. C

The following problem can be solved by 3 ÷ 1 = 3:
"Pam had 3 erasers. She gave 1 eraser each to some friends. How many friends got an eraser?"
Total number (3 erasers) ÷ number in each group (1 eraser each) = number of groups (3 friends)

19. WR

1 × 22 = 22
Example explanation
I knew that 1 × 22 was the same as 22 × 1.
I knew that the answer to Britt's equation was 22 because the property of 1 for multiplication tells you that whenever you multiply a number by 1, the answer will always be the number.

20. B

Leela should multiply 7 × 10 = 70 and then subtract 7 from the product.
70 – 7 = 63
  9 × 7 = 63

21. C

Bill should use 8 × 9 = □ to help him solve the division fact 72 ÷ 8 = Z.
One mental strategy to use when dividing is to relate division to multiplication facts. If you know that 8 × 9 = 72 and 9 × 8 = 72, then you know that 72 ÷ 8 = 9.

22. D

The best estimate is that Lucas's dad bought about 300 cobs of corn.

One bag of corn is equal to 2 baskets of corn.
23 × 2 = 46

Since 46 is close to 50, multiply 50 by 6 to get an estimate of how many cobs of corn are in 6 bags.
50 × 6 = 300

23. B

The following mathematical statement is **true**:
7 × 105 = (7 × 100) + (7 × 5)

In the number 105, there is 1 hundred, 0 tens, and 5 ones.
105 = 100 + 5

Applying the distributive property of multiplication, multiply 100 by 7 and multiply 5 by 7.

Add the products.
700 + 35 = 735

24. B

The product of 508 multiplied by 2 is 1 016.

Example strategy
  508 = 500 + 8
2 × 508 = (2 × 500) + (2 × 8)
2 × 508 = 1 000 + 16
2 × 508 = 1 016

25. C

The following array shows how the elephants were grouped for the move:

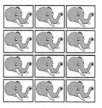

The array shows a total of 12 elephants with 3 elephants in each of the 4 rows.
12 ÷ 3 = 4

26. D

The pattern of numbers that could help Roxie divide by 8 is 72, 64, 56, 48…

The pattern of numbers starts at 72 (72 ÷ 8 = 9) and then subtracts 8 each time.

Repeated subtraction (counting backward) is one way of showing division.

72 – 8 = 64   (72 ÷ 8 = 9)
64 – 8 = 56   (64 ÷ 8 = 8)
56 – 8 = 48   (56 ÷ 8 = 7)
48 – 8 = 40   (48 ÷ 8 = 6)

27. B

There were 96 pretzels and they were shared equally among 4 children, so each child got 24 mini pretzels.

96 ÷ 4 = 24

28. 3

Leon donated 3 comics to the school library.

To solve this problem, you need to divide 59 by 7 to find how many comic books each of the seven friends got.

When you divide 59 by 7, you will have a remainder. The remainder is the number of comics that cannot be equally shared and that Leon donates to the library.

59 ÷ 7 = 8 R3

29. B

The shaded part of this diagram represents the fraction $\frac{9}{10}$.

To represent the fraction $\frac{9}{10}$, the diagram must have 10 parts in all, with 9 of the parts shaded.

30. A

The fraction $\frac{1}{6}$ is less than the fraction $\frac{3}{6}$.

Since the denominators are the same, compare the numerators.

Since 1 is less than 3, $\frac{1}{6}$ is less than $\frac{3}{6}$. $\left(\frac{1}{6} < \frac{3}{6}\right)$

31. B

The set of fractions $\frac{9}{10}, \frac{6}{10}, \frac{5}{10}$ are ordered from greatest to least.

- When the denominators of fractions are the same, compare the numerators.
- The greater the numerator, the greater the fraction.

Since 9 is greater than 6 and 6 is greater than 5, then

$\frac{9}{10} > \frac{6}{10}$ and $\frac{6}{10} > \frac{5}{10}$.

32. D

This set of fractions is ordered from least to greatest:

$\frac{1}{6}, \frac{1}{5}, \frac{1}{3}, \frac{1}{2}$

When the numerators of the fractions are the same, compare the denominators. The larger the denominator, the smaller the fraction.

To order the fractions from least to greatest, order the denominators from greatest value (6) to least value (2).

6, 5, 3, 2.

33.

$\frac{4}{10}$ represents the number of pencils that are circled.

There are 10 pencils altogether, so the denominator is 10. The circle is around 4 pencils, so 4 is the numerator.

34. WR

Tessa is correct.

$$\frac{1}{3} > \frac{1}{5}$$

Example explanation
When both numerators are 1, you need to compare the denominators. The rule is "the smaller the denominator, the greater the fraction."

Since 3 is greater than 5, then $\frac{1}{3}$ is greater than $\frac{1}{5}$.

35. B

The decimal number that Cara showed on the hundredths chart is 0.05.

There are 5 squares shaded out of a total of 100 squares (five-hundredths).

36. C

The white parts of this figure represents the decimal 0.6.

To represent the decimal 0.6, the figure must have 10 equal parts, with 6 of the parts being white.

37. A

The decimal number 0.38 can be represented by 3 dimes and 8 pennies.

Since there are 10 dimes in one dollar, you can use 3 dimes to represent 30 cents (thirty-hundredths or three-tenths).

Since there are 100 pennies in one dollar, you can use 8 pennies to represent 8 cents (eight-hundredths).

38. A

The decimal 0.07 is related to the fraction $\frac{7}{100}$.

Both the fraction $\frac{7}{100}$ and the decimal 0.07 represent 7 squares out of 100 squares on a hundredths grid.

39. B

The decimal 0.20 represents the coloured squares Chris coloured.

Chris coloured 20 squares out of 100 squares (twenty-hundredths).

40. D

A strategy that can be used to find the total cost of the books is $7.00 + $6.00 – $0.03.

Example strategy
Add 2 cents to $6.98 to make it an even $7.00.

Add 1 cent to $5.99 to make it an even $6.00.

Add the two even numbers:
$7.00 + $6.00 = $13.00

Subtract the 3 cents that was added on to make even numbers.
$13.00 – $0.03 = $12.97
$6.98 + $5.99 = $12.97

41. C

This problem, 250.25 + 99.75, has an estimated sum of 350.

Example strategy
Round the decimal numbers to the nearest whole numbers.
250.25 → 250
99.75 → 100

Add the two estimated numbers.
250 + 100 = 350

42. C

Brian earned $250.73 for the animal shelter.
$161.83 + $88.90 = $250.73

43. 6.35

Rosa bought 6.35 m of ribbon in total.

Since 4.6 is a decimal in the tenths and 1.75 is a decimal in the hundredths, you can add a 0 to the right of the 6 in 4.6 to read as 4.60.

Add the two decimal numbers.
4.60 + 1.75 = 6.35

NOTES

PATTERNS AND RELATIONS

Table of Correlations			
Outcome	Practice Questions	Unit Test Questions	Practice Test
4PR1.0 Use patterns to describe the world and to solve problems			
4PR1.1 *Identify and describe patterns found in tables and charts.*	1, 2, 3, 4	1, 2, 3, 4	20, 21
4PR1.2 *Translate among different representations of a pattern, such as a table, a chart or concrete materials.*	5	5	22
4PR1.3 *Represent, describe and extend patterns and relationships, using charts and tables, to solve problems.*	6, 7, 8, 9, 10	6, 7, 8, 9	23
4PR1.4 *Identify and explain mathematical relationships, using charts and diagrams, to solve problems.*	11, 12, 13	10	24
4PR2.0 Represent algebraic expressions in multiple ways			
4PR2.5 *Express a given problem as an equation in which a symbol is used to represent an unknown number.*	14, 15, 16, 17, 18	11, 12, 13, 14	25, 26
4PR2.6 *Solve one-step equations involving a symbol to represent an unknown number.*	19, 20, 21, 22, 23	15, 16, 17, 18	27

4PR1.1 *Identify and describe patterns found in tables and charts.*

IDENTIFYING AND DESCRIBING PATTERNS

The types of patterns usually seen in charts and tables are **number patterns**.

Number patterns often involve mathematical operations like addition, subtraction, multiplication, or division. Some patterns may involve more than one operation.

⁚Example

Addition pattern: In the number pattern 2, 7, 12, 17, the number 5 is added to each number to get the next number.

Subtraction pattern: In the number pattern 20, 16, 12, 8, the number 4 is subtracted from each number to get the next number.

Multiplication pattern: In the number pattern 2, 4, 8, 16, each number is multiplied by 2 to get the next number.

Division pattern: In the number pattern 27, 9, 3, 1, each number is divided by 3 to get the next number.

Mixed pattern: In the number pattern 5, 7, 6, 8, 7, the number 2 is added to the first number to get the second number. The number 1 is subtracted from the second number to get the third number. The pattern continues, adding 2 then subtracting 1.

Number patterns can increase, decrease, or repeat.

⁚Example

Increasing pattern: In the number pattern 5, 10, 15, 20, the numbers get larger in value. A pattern that increases is sometimes called a growing pattern.

Decreasing pattern: In the number pattern 19, 17, 15, 13, the numbers get smaller in value. A pattern that decreases is sometimes called a shrinking pattern.

Repeating pattern: In the number pattern 5, 3, 5, 3, the set of numbers that keeps repeating is 5, 3.

Patterns can be described by how they are made. The method used to make a pattern is often referred to as the **pattern rule** or the rule. For example, the number pattern 4, 8, 16, 32 can be described by the rule *start with 4 and multiply each number by 2.*

PATTERNS IN TABLES AND CHARTS

It is often easier to see relationships between numbers in a pattern when the numbers are presented in a chart or table. Once you identify the relationships between the numbers (determine the rule), you can identify patterns, find missing numbers, and identify errors.

Example

Number of Scooters in the Group	Total Number of Wheels
1	2
2	4
3	6
4	?

Using the pattern of numbers in the given table, how many wheels are there in total when there are 4 scooters?

Step 1
Examine how the number of wheels changes each time another scooter is included.

- The number of wheels increases by 2 each time.
- The pattern rule is "add 2 to each number" to get the next number.

Step 2
Apply the pattern rule.
6 + 2 = 8
There will be a total of 8 wheels on four scooters.

1	2	3	4	5	6	7	⑧	9	10
11	12	13	14	15	16	⑰	18	19	20
21	22	23	24	25	㉖	27	28	29	30
31	32	33	34	㉟	36	37	38	39	40
41	42	43	㊹	45	46	47	48	49	50
51	52	㊾	54	55	56	57	58	59	60
61	㉒	63	64	65	66	67	68	69	70
㉑	72	73	74	75	76	77	78	79	80

Starting at the number 8, what is the pattern rule for the circled numbers on the given hundred chart?

Starting at 8, the number 9 is added to each number to get the next number.

   8 + 9 = 17
17 + 9 = 26
26 + 9 = 35
    etc.

Example

The circled numbers on the given multiplication chart make a pattern.

X	0	1	2	3	4
0	0	0	0	0	0
1	⓪	①	②	③	④
2	0	2	4	6	8
3	0	3	6	9	12
4	0	4	8	12	16

How was this pattern of numbers made?

The pattern of circled numbers was made by multiplying each top number by 1 to get the circled number.

$0 \times 1 = 0$
$1 \times 1 = 1$
$1 \times 2 = 2$
     etc.

Use the following information to answer the next question.

Karl created a pattern on a multiplication chart when he circled the following numbers.

×	0	1	2	3	4	5	6
0	0	0	0	0	0	0	0
1	0	1	2	3	4	5	6
2	0	2	4	6	8	10	12
3	0	3	6	9	12	15	18
4	0	4	8	12	16	20	24
5	⓪	⑤	⑩	⑮	⑳	㉕	㉚
6	0	6	12	18	24	30	36

1. Karl created this pattern by multiplying each number in the top row by
   A. 1   B. 2
   C. 5   D. 10

Use the following information to answer the next question.

The following chart shows four patterns of numbers.

Pattern A	1	10	19		
Pattern B	3	12	21		
Pattern C	4	13	22		
Pattern D	6	15	24		

2. The number 37 belongs to

    A. Pattern A   B. Pattern B

    C. Pattern C   D. Pattern D

Use the following information to answer the next question.

Thomas sees this pattern of numbers in one row of a multiplication chart.

32	40	48	56	64	72

3. The pattern rule for the given set of numbers is

    A. multiply each number by 8 to get the next number

    B. multiply each number by 6 to get the next number

    C. add 8 to each number to get the next number

    D. add 9 to each number to get the next number

Use the following information to answer the next question.

Jessie creates the number pattern in the following chart. She leaves two numbers out. She asks her friend to figure out which two numbers should replace the symbols @ and #.

3	5	7	3
3	5	7	5
3	5	7	7
3	5	@	#

4. In order, the two numbers that replace the symbols @ and # are

A. 3 and 3

B. 5 and 7

C. 7 and 3

D. 7 and 7

4PR1.2 *Translate among different representations of a pattern, such as a table, a chart or concrete materials.*

REPRODUCING A PATTERN FOUND IN A TABLE

The same pattern can be displayed using different methods. For example, you can take a pattern found in a chart or table and reproduce it using concrete materials like tiles, counting chips, or blocks.

- First you need to find the rule that describes the number pattern shown in the chart.
- Then you need to use the same rule when you build your pattern using concrete materials.

The relationship between the pattern in the table and its concrete representation stays the same because the same pattern rule was followed.

:Example

Kirby makes the given chart to show the number of counting chips she will use to make a growing pattern of five different figures.

The pattern can be described as starting with 1 chip and then adding 1 more chip, then 2 more chips, then 3 more chips, and then 4 more chips as each figure is made.
The pattern rule can be described as +1, +2, +3, +4.

Figure	Number of Chips
1	1
2	2
3	4
4	7
5	11

Kirby then builds the figures out of actual counting chips using the same pattern rule of +1, +2, +3, +4.

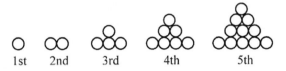

The number of counting chips in the chart is the same as the number of chips used in the building of the concrete pattern.

Use the following information to answer the next question.

Dorie sees the given pattern of numbers in a table. She uses square pattern blocks to create the same pattern.

Row 1	1
Row 2	2
Row 3	4
Row 4	7

5. Which set of squares represents the pattern of numbers displayed in the given table?

A.

Row 1	
Row 2	
Row 3	
Row 4	

B.

Row 1	
Row 2	
Row 3	
Row 4	

C.

Row 1	
Row 2	
Row 3	
Row 4	

D.

Row 1	
Row 2	
Row 3	
Row 4	

4PR1.3 *Represent, describe and extend patterns and relationships, using charts and tables, to solve problems.*

SOLVING PROBLEMS USING PATTERNS IN CHARTS AND TABLES

To solve problems using patterns, you first need to identify the relationships among the numbers being used. Once you understand how the numbers change, you will then be able to:

- identify patterns
- translate patterns into charts or tables
- extend patterns

EXTENDING PATTERNS

To extend a pattern means to continue a pattern by applying the pattern rule.

:Example

Megan is creating a design using coloured tiles. The different numbers of coloured tiles she is using create a pattern.

The given chart shows the number of different coloured tiles she has used so far. If the pattern of numbers continues, how many yellow tiles will Megan be using?

Colour of Tiles	Number of Tiles Used
Red	1
Blue	5
Green	9
Black	13
Orange	?
Yellow	?

To solve this problem, you first need to determine the relationship between the numbers (figure out how the numbers are changing).

The pattern starts with one red tile, then the number of each colour of tile increases by 4. (1 + 4 = 5), (5 + 4 = 9), (9 + 4 = 13)

To extend the pattern, use the same pattern rule and add 4 to each number to get the next number.
Orange: 13 + 4 = 17
Yellow: 17 + 4 = 21

If the pattern continues, Megan will use 21 yellow tiles.

TRANSLATING PATTERNS INTO CHARTS OR TABLES

You can take a pattern that is written in words or take a pattern rule, then make a chart to display the pattern. When you make the chart, be sure to follow the pattern rule or description carefully and accurately.

Example

Mr. Canyon asked his students to make a chart or table showing the following pattern description "start with the number 63 and subtract 7 for four counts."

To solve this problem, the first number in your table must be 63. Then you need to subtract 7 four times. This means that you will have 4 numbers following the number 63, a total of five numbers in all. Be sure to label the chart.

Start	1st	2nd	3rd	4th
63	56	49	42	35

Use the following information to answer the next question.

Mr. Landon asked four of his students to make charts representing the pattern rule "add 2, then add 1; repeat."

6. The chart that represents the given pattern rule is

A.
1st	2nd	3rd	4th	5th
9	11	10	12	11

B.
1st	2nd	3rd	4th	5th
13	15	16	18	19

C.
1st	2nd	3rd	4th	5th
16	18	19	21	23

D.
1st	2nd	3rd	4th	5th
20	22	23	24	26

Use the following information to answer the next question.

Daria wants to find what the 4th number is in the following pattern:

1st	2nd	3rd	4th	5th
635	625	615	?	595

Before she can do this, she needs to identify how the numbers in the pattern change.

7. The pattern rule that explains how the numbers change is to start at 635 and
   A. add 1 each time
   B. add 10 each time
   C. subtract 1 each time
   D. subtract 10 each time

Use the following information to answer the next question.

In Mr. Jacob's math class, students are asked to create problems that the class will solve.

The following chart shows a pattern of numbers that Ayla made for the class to complete.

1st	2nd	3rd	4th	5th	6th
?	?	121	131	141	151

8. The first two numbers of Ayla's pattern are

    A. 100 and 110   **B.** 100 and 111

    C. 101 and 110   **D.** 101 and 111

Use the following information to answer the next question.

Nila drew five different polygons. She made this chart to show the number of sides each polygon had.

Polygon	Number of Sides
1	3
2	4
3	6
4	9
5	13

9. The pattern rule Nila used when she drew the polygons was to

    A. add 1, then 2, then 4, then 5 more sides

    B. add 1, then 2, then 1, then 2 more sides

    C. add 1, then 2, then 3, then 4 more sides

    D. add 1, then 2, then 3, then 5 more sides

Use the following information to answer the next question.

The following chart shows the amount of money students collected for an animal shelter.

Mon	Tue	Wed	Thu	Fri	Sat	Sun
$2	$4	$8	$16	$32	?	?

10. If the pattern continues, how much money will the students collect on Sunday?

A. $64

B. $86

C. $128

D. $138

4PR1.4 *Identify and explain mathematical relationships, using charts and diagrams, to solve problems.*

USING CHARTS AND DIAGRAMS TO SOLVE PROBLEMS

You can use charts and certain kinds of diagrams to show mathematical relationships. Two of the diagrams that are commonly used to show relationships are Carroll diagrams and Venn diagrams.

CARROLL DIAGRAMS

A **Carroll diagram** is a type of table that can be used to arrange information in an organized way in order to solve a problem that involves two or more choices.

When using a Carroll diagram, check marks (✓) and *X*s can be used to help you keep track of the information as you read through the problem.
The check mark (✓) represents **yes** and the *X* represents **no**.

Example

Tom, Alex, and Emma each have a different favourite sandwich: egg salad, ham, and grilled cheese.

- Neither Alex nor Emma like egg salad sandwiches.
- Tom is allergic to ham, so he never eats ham sandwiches.

This is how you can use a Carroll diagram to solve the problem of which favourite sandwich belongs to each person.

- Put an *X* under "egg salad" for both Alex and Emma, since they do not like egg salad. That means Tom's favourite sandwich must be egg salad. Put a ✓ under "egg salad" for Tom.
- Put an *X* under both "ham" and "grilled cheese" for Tom because you now know that his favourite sandwich is egg salad.
- Since Alex never eats ham, put an *X* under "ham" for Alex. That means that Alex's favourite sandwich must be grilled cheese. Put a ✓ under "grilled cheese" for Alex.
- That leaves the ham sandwich for Emma.

	Egg salad	Ham	Grilled Cheese
Tom	✓	X	X
Alex	X	X	✓
Emma	X	✓	X

Tom's favourite sandwich is egg salad, Alex's favourite sandwich is grilled cheese, and Emma's favourite sandwich is ham.

VENN DIAGRAMS

A **Venn diagram** is a diagram that is made up of at least two circles or ovals. Each shape represents a different set of information and is labelled to show what information it represents.

- The two labels make up the sorting rule.
- If the shapes do not overlap, none of the information given is common to the two groups.
- If the shapes do overlap, the information inside the area where the shapes overlap is described by both labels.

Example

Use a Venn diagram to show the relationships among these numbers:
2, 6, 8, 10, 11, 18, 19, 37, 43

Step 1
The sorting rule that should be used is 2-digit numbers or even numbers.
Label one circle "2-Digit Numbers" and the other circle "Even Numbers."

Step 2
Place all the 2-digit numbers that are **not** even in the circle that is labelled "2-Digit Numbers."
11, 19, 37, 43

Step 3
Place all the even numbers that are **not** 2-digit numbers in the circle labelled "Even Numbers."
2, 6, 8

Step 4
Place the numbers that are both even and 2-digit inside the overlapped part.
10, 18

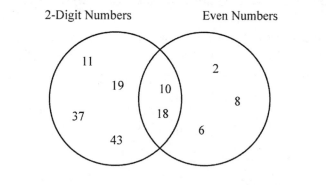

A set may consist of a limited number of objects, such as the set of prime numbers less than 120. A set can also be an infinite number of objects, such as the set of real numbers.

Venn diagrams are diagrams illustrate the relationships between sets. A **set** is a collection of particular objects (or elements).

Example

Use shading in a Venn diagram to illustrate the set of boys who play football but not hockey.

This operator describes the set of boys who play one sport only, which is football in this case. The region to be shaded is the circle representing the set of football players without shading the region that is also part of the hockey circle.

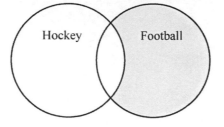

Venn diagrams represent sets that may have common elements.

Use shading in a Venn diagram to illustrate the boys who play hockey or football.

This Venn diagram consists of two overlapping circles that illustrate the two sets of boys who play each sport. The overlapping region represents the set of boys who play both sports.

The set of boys who play hockey or football consists of all the boys who play only one of the two sports plus the boys who play both sports. All three regions shaded represent the set of boys who play both sports.

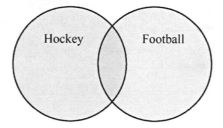

In a particular sports school for boys, every boy participates in at least one of the two sports being offered: hockey and football.

Use shading in a Venn diagram to illustrate the boys who play hockey and football.

The set of boys who play hockey and football is illustrated in the Venn diagram by the overlapping region of the two circles, so only this region is shaded.

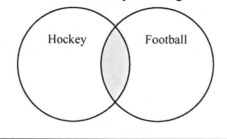

Use the following information to answer the next question.

Yuka asks some students if they play baseball or soccer in the summer. She draws this diagram to show the results.

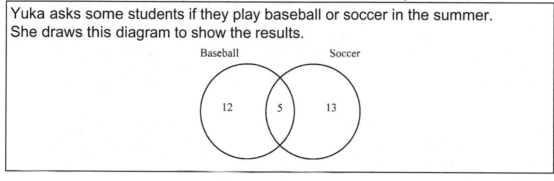

11. The number of students who play soccer in the summer is

A. 5   B. 8

C. 13   D. 18

Use the following information to answer the next question.

Suri sorts the numbers from 1 to 20 by putting them into a sorting chart.

12. Which of the following charts shows the numbers sorted correctly?

A.

	Less than 10	10 or greater
Even	2, 4, 6, 8, 10	12, 14, 16, 18, 20
Odd	1, 3, 5, 7, 9	11, 13, 15, 17, 19

B.

	Less than 10	10 or greater
Even	2, 4, 6, 8,	10, 12, 14, 16, 18, 20
Odd	1, 3, 5, 7	11, 13, 15, 17, 19

C.

	Less than 10	10 or greater
Even	2, 4, 6, 8	10, 12, 14, 16, 18, 20
Odd	1, 3, 5, 7, 9	11, 13, 15, 17, 19

D.

	Less than 10	10 or greater
Even	2, 4, 6, 8	10, 12, 14, 16, 18
Odd	1, 3, 5, 7, 9	11, 13, 15, 17, 19

Use the following information to answer the next question.

Carlo, Maria, Andy, and Rafi each have a different favourite sport: volleyball, hockey, skiing, and soccer.

- Carlo and Andy do not like volleyball.
- Rafi often goes to the mountain for his favourite sport.
- Andy likes to run.

Written Response

13. What is the favourite sport of each student?

Complete the given Carroll diagram by entering the data into the correct squares to solve this problem.
Use a checkmark ✓ to represent *yes* and the letter X to represent *no*.

	Volleyball	Hockey	Skiing	Soccer
Carlo				
Maria				
Andy				
Rafi				

4PR2.5 *Express a given problem as an equation in which a symbol is used to represent an unknown number.*

USING SYMBOLS FOR THE UNKNOWN IN EQUATIONS

Symbols can be signs, letters, or shapes used to represent mathematical concepts.

Example

- The symbol = represents the words *is equal to*. For example, 5 × 3 = 15.
- The symbol < represents the words *less than*. For example, 8 < 11.
- The symbol °C represents the words *degrees Celsius*.
- For example, the temperature is 7°C.

USING AN EQUATION

An **equation** is a number sentence that uses the equal sign (=) to show that the amount on each side of the equal sign has the same value.

3 + 5 = 8
    8 = 8

An equation is always written horizontally. If the numbers are written vertically, it is not considered to be an equation.

Equation	Not an Equation
2 × 8 = 16	8 × 2 16

USING SYMBOLS FOR UNKNOWNS

In a problem, there is always an unknown. An unknown is what you are trying to find out by performing some type of operation (the solution to the problem).

A problem can be written in equation form and the unknown expressed as a symbol, like a letter, question mark, or shape. The unknown can come anywhere in the equation.

For example, 2 + 3 = *N* or 2 + ? = 5 or □ + 3 = 5.

⋰Example

Lily picked some apples from the apple tree in her backyard. After she gave her neighbour 14 apples, Lily had 9 apples left.
How many apples did Lily pick from the apple tree?

To solve this problem, you can let the letter *A* represent the unknown, which is the number of apples that Lily picked. Following are two equations that you can write to express this problem.
$A - 14 = 9$
$A = 14 + 9$
In each equation, the letter *A* represents the same unknown, which is the 23 apples that Lily picked from the tree.

⋰Example

This pictorial representation shows that there are 3 rows of apples with 4 apples in each row. The unknown in this problem is how many apples there are in total.

To write an equation for this problem, first determine the symbol that will represent the total number of apples. For example, let □ represent the total number of apples picked.

Following are some of the equations that can be used to solve this problem.
$3 \times 4 = \square$
$4 \times 3 = \square$
$3 + 3 + 3 + 3 = \square$
$4 + 4 + 4 = \square$
$\square = 3 \times 4$
$\square = 4 \times 3$

Use the following information to answer the next question.

Shalu has 28 star stickers. She plans to paste an equal number of stickers on 4 different pages. She needs to find how many stickers she should paste on each page.

14. If *m* represents the number of stickers that Shalu should paste on each page, then which of the following equations will solve Shalu's problem?

A. $4 \times 28 = m$ B. $28 \div 4 = m$

C. $m \div 4 = 28$ D. $28 - m = 4$

Use the following information to answer the next question.

Miss Wilson types 40 words in 1 minute on the computer.

15. Which of the following equations can be used to find how many words Miss Wilson can type in 3 minutes?

A. $40 \times 3 = W$ B. $40 \times 1 = W$

C. $1 \times W = 40$ D. $W \times 3 = 40$

Use the following information to answer the next question.

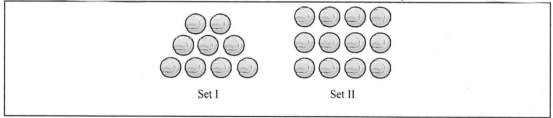

Set I   Set II

16. Which of the following equations **best** represents the two sets of tennis balls?

A. $? = 9 + 12$ B. $? = 9 \times 12$

C. $? = 21 - 3$ D. $? = 21 \div 3$

17. Which of the following problems can be solved using the equation $Z - 45 = 5$?
    A. Mya opened a bag of chips and ate 45 chips. There were 5 chips left. How many chips were in the bag to begin with?

    B. Sam had 5 bags of marbles. Each bag had 45 marbles. How many marbles did he have in all?

    C. Yuka baked 45 cookies. She gave 5 cookies to her sister. How many cookies are left?

    D. Jill picked 45 tulips. She put 5 tulips in each vase. How many vases did she use?

Use the following information to answer the next question.

Justin is asked to find the total number of sides in 12 triangles. To solve this problem, he uses an equation in which the letter Y represents the total number of sides.

18. Which of the following equations can Justin use to solve the problem?
    A. $3 + 12 = Y$ B. $12 \div Y = 3$
    C. $Y = 3 \times 12$ D. $3 \times Y = 12$

4PR2.6 *Solve one-step equations involving a symbol to represent an unknown number.*

SOLVING PROBLEMS THAT USE SYMBOLS

When you solve problems that use symbols, you can use inverse (opposite) operations or related facts to help you determine the answer.

Adding and subtracting are inverse operations. For example, $2 + 3 = 5$ and $5 - 3 = 2$.

Multiplying and dividing are inverse operations. For example, $2 \times 4 = 8$ and $8 \div 4 = 2$.

In related facts, you can add or multiply the numbers in any order and the answer will still be the same. For example, $5 \times 6 = 30$ and $6 \times 5 = 30$.

Example

What is the value of N in the equation $15 + N = 25$?

To solve this addition problem, you can use the inverse operation of subtraction.
$$15 + N = 25$$
$$N = 25 - 15$$
$$N = 10$$
$$15 + 10 = 25$$

Example

Mr. Adams buys 2 packages of felt pens that have the same number of pens in each package. He has 24 felt pens in total.
How many pens are in each package?

The equation $2 \times Z = 24$ can be used to find the number of felt pens in each package.
To solve this multiplication problem, you can use the inverse operation of division.

$2 \times Z = 24$
$Z = 24 \div 2$
$Z = 12$
$2 \times 12 = 24$

There were 12 felt pens in each package.

Use the following information to answer the next question.

> Bert has a bag of nine candies. He eats four of the candies at recess time.
> Bert writes an equation in which T represents the number of candies that he now has.
> $4 + T = 9$

19. The value of T in Bert's equation is
    A. 2   B. 5
    C. 13   D. 36

20. In the equation $Z = 14 \times 6$, the letter Z represents the number
    A. 24   B. 34
    C. 64   D. 84

Use the following information to answer the next question.

> Pryia had a total of 31 stuffed animals. She kept her 12 favourite stuffed animals and gave the rest to her cousin. In the following equation, the letter Y represents the number of stuffed animals Pryia gave to her cousin.
> $Y + 12 = 31$

21. How many stuffed animals did Pryia give to her cousin?
    A. 43   B. 29
    C. 21   D. 19

Use the following information to answer the next question.

Essa placed 96 marbles into 8 bags, placing an equal number in each bag.

22. If the letter *B* represents the number of marbles placed in each bag, which of the following equations can be used to solve the problem?

    A. $96 = B \div 8$ B. $96 \div B = 8$

    C. $8 = B \times 96$ D. $96 \times 8 = B$

Numerical Response

23. In the equation $4 \times M = 92$, the letter *M* represents the unknown number.

The letter *M* represents the number _____.

Answers and Solutions
Patterns and Relations

1. C	6. B	11. D	16. A	21. D
2. A	7. D	12. C	17. A	22. B
3. C	8. D	13. WR	18. C	23. 23
4. C	9. C	14. B	19. B	
5. B	10. C	15. A	20. D	

1. C

Karl multiplied each number in the top row by 5.
0 × 5 = 0, 1 × 5 = 5,
2 × 5 = 10, 3 × 5 = 15…

2. A

The number 37 belongs to Pattern A.

The rule in Pattern A is
"add 9 to each number" to get the next number.
1 + 9 = 10, 10 + 9 = 19,
19 + 9 = 28, 28 + 9 = 37

The pattern for choice B is
3, 21, 30, and 39

The pattern for choice C is
4, 13, 22, 31, and 40

The pattern for choice D is
6, 15, 24, 33, and 42

3. C

The pattern rule for the given set of numbers is "add 8 to each number to get the next number."
32 + 8 = 40, 40 + 8 = 48, 48 + 8 = 56…

4. C

In order, the numbers that replace the symbols @ and # are 7 and 3.

Row 1: 3, 5, 7, 3 (repeat the first number in column four)
Row 2: 3, 5, 7, 5 (repeat the second number in column four)
Row 3: 3, 5, 7, 7 (repeat the third number in column four)
Row 4: 3, 5, 7, 3 (repeat the first number in column four)

5. B

This set of squares represents the pattern of numbers displayed in the given table:

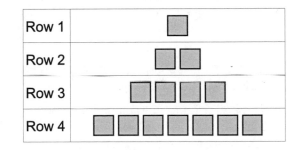

Row 1		
Row 2		
Row 3		
Row 4		

Row 1 has 1 square.
Row 2 has 2 squares.
Row 3 has 4 squares.
Row 4 has 7 squares.

6. B

The following chart represents the pattern rule "add 2, then add 1; repeat."

1st	2nd	3rd	4th	5th
13	15	16	18	19

13 + 2 = 1515 + 1 = 16, repeat
16 + 2 = 1818 + 1 = 19

7. D

The pattern rule is "start at 635 and subtract 10 each time."
(635 − 10 = 625), (625 − 10 = 615),
(615 − 10 = 605), (605 − 10 = 595)

8. D

The first two numbers of Ayla's pattern are 101 and 111.

From 121 to 151, the pattern rule is add 10 each time.

Since the missing numbers are at the beginning of the pattern, you need to subtract 10 each time to find the first two numbers.
121 − 10 = 111 and 111 − 10 = 101

9. C

The pattern rule Nila used was "add 1, then 2, then 3, then 4 more sides."
3 + 1 = 4, 4 + 2 = 6, 6 + 3 = 9, 9 + 4 = 13

10. C

If the pattern continues, the students will collect $128 on Sunday.

The pattern rule is "multiply each number by 2" to get the next number.
32 × 2 = 64 (Saturday)
64 × 2 = 128 (Sunday)

11. D

There is a total of 18 students who play soccer in the summer.

Thirteen students play only soccer and 5 students play both soccer and baseball.
13 + 5 = 18

12. C

The following chart shows the numbers sorted correctly:

	Less than 10	10 or greater
Even	2, 4, 6, 8	10, 12, 14, 16, 18, 20
Odd	1, 3, 5, 7, 9	11, 13, 15, 17, 19

All the even numbers are in the top row:
2, 4, 6, and 8 are less than ten
10, 12, 14, 16, 18, and 20 are ten or greater

All the odd numbers are in the bottom row:
1, 3, 5, 7, and 9 are less than ten
11, 13, 15, 17, and 19 are greater than ten

13. WR

Step 1
Carlo and Andy do not like volleyball.

	Volleyball	Hockey	Skiing	Soccer
Carlo	X			
Maria				
Andy	X			
Rafi				

Step 2
Rafi often goes to the mountains for his favourite sport. The only mountain sport listed is skiing.

	Volleyball	Hockey	Skiing	Soccer
Carlo	X		X	
Maria			X	
Andy	X		X	
Rafi	X	X	✓	X

Step 3
Andy likes to run. The only sport with a lot of running is soccer.

	Volleyball	Hockey	Skiing	Soccer
Carlo	X		X	X
Maria			X	X
Andy	X	X	X	✓
Rafi	X	X	✓	X

Step 4
The only sport that remains free for Carlo is hockey.

	Volleyball	Hockey	Skiing	Soccer
Carlo	X	✓	X	X
Maria		X	X	X
Andy	X	X	X	✓
Rafi	X	X	✓	X

Step 5
Maria's favourite sport is volleyball.

	Volleyball	Hockey	Skiing	Soccer
Carlo	X	✓	X	X
Maria	✓	X	X	X
Andy	X	X	X	✓
Rafi	X	X	✓	X

14. B

The equation $28 ÷ 4 = m$ will solve Shalu's problem.

Total number ÷ number of groups
  = number in each group
$28 ÷ 4 = m$
$28 ÷ 4 = 7$
  $m = 7$

15. A

The equation $40 × 3 = W$ can be used to find how many words Miss Wilson can type in 3 minutes.

Number of words per minute × number of minutes = number of words in 3 minutes
$40 × 3 = W$
$40 × 3 = 120$
  $W = 120$

16. A

The equation that best represents the two sets of tennis balls is $? = 9 + 12$.

There are 9 tennis balls in Set I and 12 tennis balls in Set II.
The symbol ? represents the total number of tennis balls.
 $? = 9 + 12$
$21 = 9 + 12$
 $? = 21$

17. A

The letter Z represents the unknown. In the case of Mya opening a bag of chips, the total number of chips in the bag is unknown.

She ate 45 chips, which means take away 45 or -45.

After eating the chips, there were 5 chips left in the bag, which is equal to 5 or $= 5$.

The problem can be solved by using the equation $Z - 45 = 5$.
$Z - 45 = 5$
  $Z = 45 + 5$
  $Z = 50$

18. C

The equation that Justin can use to solve the problem is $Y = 3 × 12$.

Each triangle has 3 sides. There are 12 triangles. To find the unknown, which is the total number of sides, Justin needs to multiply 12 by 3.
 $Y = 3 × 12$
$36 = 3 × 12$
 $Y = 36$

19. B

The value of T in Bert's equation is 5.

Use the inverse operation of subtraction to find the value of T.
$4 + T = 9$
  $T = 9 - 4$
  $T = 5$

Bert now has 5 candies.

20. D

The letter Z represents the number 84.
$Z = 14 × 6$
$Z = 84$

21. D

Pryia gave 19 stuffed animals to her cousin.

Use the inverse operation of subtraction to find the value of Y.
$Y + 12 = 31$
  $Y = 31 - 12$
  $Y = 19$

22. B

The equation $96 ÷ B = 8$ can be used to solve the problem.
Total number ÷ number in each group
  = number of groups

Use related facts to help you find the value of B.

If $96 ÷ B = 8$, then $96 ÷ 8 = B$.
$96 ÷ 8 = 12$
$B = 12$
$98 ÷ 12 = 8$

Essa placed 12 marbles in each bag.

23. 23

Example strategy
Use the inverse operation of division to
solve this multiplication problem.

$4 \times M = 92$
$92 \div 4 = M$
$92 \div 4 = 23$
$M = 23$

To check your answer, replace M with 23.
$4 \times 23 = 96$

UNIT TEST

Use the following information to answer the next question.

Emma made the following number chart, but left out three numbers from the pattern.

Number Chart	
1	8
2	16
3	24
4	
5	40
6	48
7	
8	
9	72

1. In order, the three missing numbers are
   A. 32, 58, 64   B. 32, 56, 64

   C. 36, 56, 64   D. 36, 56, 68

Use the following information to answer the next question.

Marnie circled five numbers on the following chart to create a number pattern.

X	0	1	2	3	4
0	0	0	0	0	0
1	0	1	2	3	4
2	⓪	②	④	⑥	⑧
3	0	3	6	9	12
4	0	4	8	12	16

2. What did Marnie do to each number in the top row to get the circled numbers?

    A. She added 2 to each top number.

    B. She divided each top number by 2.

    C. She multiplied each top number by 1.

    D. She multiplied each top number by 2.

Use the following information to answer the next question.

David made this chart to show the number of straws he will need to make six hexagonal shapes.

Number of Shapes	Number of Straws
1	6
2	12
3	16
4	24
5	30
6	36

3. The number in the chart that does **not** follow the pattern rule David used is

    A. 16   B. 24

    C. 30   D. 42

Use the following information to answer the next question.

Starting at the number 71, Pat circled numbers on the given number chart to create a pattern.

1	2	3	4	5	6	7	⑧	9	10
11	12	13	14	15	16	⑰	18	19	20
21	22	23	24	25	㉖	27	28	29	30
31	32	33	34	㉟	36	37	38	39	40
41	42	43	㊹	45	46	47	48	49	50
51	52	㊳	54	55	56	57	58	59	60
61	㉒	63	64	65	66	67	68	69	70
㋑	72	73	74	75	76	77	78	79	80

4. Which of the following statements describes the circled pattern of numbers, starting at the number 71?

   A. The ones increase by 1, and the tens increase by 1.

   B. The ones increase by 1, and the tens decrease by 1.

   C. The ones decrease by 1, and the tens increase by 1.

   D. The ones decrease by 1, and the tens decrease by 1.

Use the following information to answer the next question.

The number pattern in the following chart represents the number of pencils found on the floor in a classroom.

Day	Pencils
Monday	2
Tuesday	4
Wednesday	3
Thursday	5
Friday	4

Jessie used building blocks to represent the given pattern of numbers displayed in the chart.

5. The set of building blocks that represents the given pattern of numbers is

A.

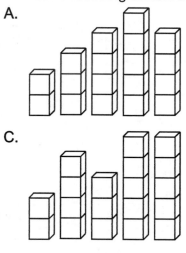

B.

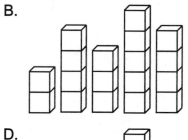

C.

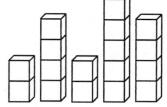

D.

Use the following information to answer the next question.

Ari makes a table to show the number of straws he used to build some bridges.

Bridge	Straws
1	87
2	94
3	101
4	?
5	?
6	?

6. If the pattern continues, how many straws will Ari need to build the 6th bridge?

   A. 132   B. 129

   C. 125   D. 122

Use the following information to answer the next question.

In a Grade Four class, the math problem for the day is to write a list of four numbers that follow the pattern rule
"add 8 each time".

7. Which of the following charts follows the given rule?

A.

1	2	3	4
87	95	103	111

B.

1	2	3	4
89	97	104	112

C.

1	2	3	4
91	99	106	124

D.

1	2	3	4
93	100	108	116

Use the following information to answer the next question.

Kate's class practises math facts every day of the week. The given chart displays the number of facts they practised from Monday to Wednesday this week.

Monday	5
Tuesday	10
Wednesday	20
Thursday	?
Friday	?

8. If the pattern continues, in order, how many facts will the class practise on Thursday and Friday?

   A. 25 and 50   B. 30 and 40

   C. 40 and 60   D. 40 and 80

| Written Response |

9. Start at 45 and make a pattern of numbers for five counts. Show your pattern of numbers in the chart below. Explain the pattern rule you used.

1st	2nd	3rd	4th	5th	6th
45					

10. Carrie, Joe, John, and Amy like to drink chocolate milk at lunch.

    Amy, Joe, Ellen, and Kel like to drink white milk at lunch.

    Which of the following diagrams shows the information given about the drinks the children like?

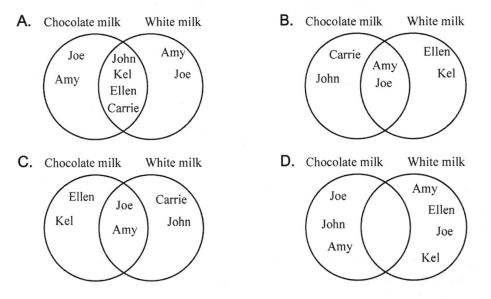

11. Ryder buys 6 bags of marbles with the same number of marbles in each bag. He has 54 marbles altogether. How many marbles are in each bag?

    If R represents the number of marbles in each bag, which of the following equations can be used to solve the problem?

    A. $R \div 6 = 54$ B. $6 = R \div 54$

    C. $6 \times R = 54$ D. $R = 54 \times 6$

Use the following information to answer the next question.

There were 19 apples in a basket. Leena puts more apples into the basket. There are now a total of 28 apples in the basket. How many apples did Leena put into the basket?

12. If k represents the number of apples Leena put into the basket, which of the following equations can be used to solve the problem?

    A. $19 - k = 28$ B. $k - 19 = 28$

    C. $28 = k + 19$ D. $19 + 28 = k$

Use the following information to answer the next question.

At a fair, four clowns are holding the same number of balloons to give to some little children.

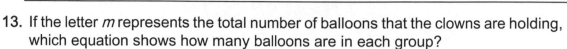

13. If the letter *m* represents the total number of balloons that the clowns are holding, which equation shows how many balloons are in each group?

A. $8 - 2 = m$

B. $8 \div 4 = m$

C. $4 + 4 = m$

D. $4 \times 2 = m$

| Written Response |

14. Conner bought 3 packages of coloured markers. He now has a total of 72 new markers. How many coloured markers were in each package?

What is the unknown in this problem?

Let *R* represent the unknown and write an equation that can be used to solve the problem.

15. What number does the letter *P* represent in the given equation, $6 + P = 18$?

A. 3   B. 8

C. 12   D. 24

16. In the equation $A + 6 = 41$, the letter A represents the number
    A. 47   B. 41
    C. 35   D. 25

Use the following information to answer the next question.

Ava had 56 pages left to read in her book. She read the same number of pages each evening until she finished reading the book. It took her 8 days to finish. In the following equation, the letter Z represents the number of pages Ava read each evening.
$56 \div Z = 8$

17. How many pages did Ava read each evening?
    A. 6   B. 7
    C. 8   D. 9

18. In the equation $45 = N + 27$, what number does the letter N represent?
    A. 18   B. 22
    C. 28   D. 72

ANSWERS AND SOLUTIONS – UNIT TEST

1. B	6. D	11. C	16. C
2. D	7. A	12. C	17. B
3. A	8. D	13. B	18. A
4. B	9. WR	14. WR	
5. B	10. B	15. C	

1. B

In order, the three missing numbers are 32, 56, 64.

The pattern rule Emma used is "add 8 to each number" to get the next number.
24 + 8 = 32, 48 + 8 = 56, 56 + 8 = 64

2. D

Marnie multiplied each number in the top row by 2 to get the circled numbers.
(0 × 2 = 0), (1 × 2 = 2), (2 × 2 = 4), (3 × 2 = 6), (4 × 2 = 8)

3. A

The number 16 does not follow David's pattern rule.

A hexagon has 6 sides, so the pattern rule is "add 6 to each number" to get the next number.
12 + 6 = 18, not 16

4. B

The statement that describes the pattern of numbers starting at 71 is the ones increase by 1, and the tens decrease by 1.

The ones increase by 1: (71, 62, 53, 44, …)

The tens decrease by 1: (71, 62, 53, 44, …)

5. B

The following set of building blocks represents the given pattern:

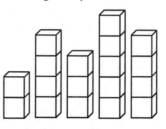

Starting at the left, the columns of building blocks are 2 blocks, 4 blocks, 3 blocks, 5 blocks, 4 blocks.

6. D

If the pattern continues, Ari will need 122 straws to build the 6th bridge.

The pattern rule is "add 7 to each number" to get the next number.
87 + 7 = 94 and 94 + 7 = 101

Bridge 4: 101 + 7 = 108
Bridge 5: 108 + 7 = 115
Bridge 6: 115 + 7 = 122

7. A

This chart follows the given rule "add 8 each time".

1	2	3	4
87	95	103	111

(87 + 8 = 95),
(95 + 8 = 103), (103 + 8 = 111)

8. D

If the pattern continues, in order, the class will practise 40 and 80 math facts on Thursday and Friday.

The pattern rule is "multiply each number by 2" to get the next number.
$5 \times 2 = 10$ and $10 \times 2 = 20$

Thursday: $20 \times 2 = 40$
Friday: $40 \times 2 = 80$

9. WR

Example pattern

1st	2nd	3rd	4th	5th	6th
45	38	31	24	17	10

Example explanation
The pattern rule I used to make this pattern of numbers is subtract 7 from each number to get the next number.

10. B

The following diagram shows the information about the drinks the children like:

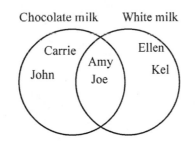

- Carrie and John only like chocolate milk, so their names go in the chocolate milk circle.
- Ellen and Kel only like white milk, so their names go in the white milk circle.
- Amy and Joe like both chocolate and white milk, so their names go in the middle where the two circles overlap.

11. C

The equation $6 \times R = 54$ can be used to solve the problem.

You can solve this multiplication problem by using the inverse operation of division.
$6 \times R = 54$
$R = 54 \div 6$
$R = 9$
$6 \times 9 = 54$

There are 9 marbles in each bag.

12. C

The equation $28 = k + 19$ can be used to solve the problem.

This equation is a "whole-part-part" problem.

- Whole: There are 28 apples in all.
- Part: k represents the number of apples Leena put into the basket.
- Part: 19 apples were in the basket before Leena put her apples in.

The problem can be solved using the inverse operation of subtraction.
$28 - 19 = k$
$k = 9$

Leena put 9 apples in the basket.

13. B

The equation that shows the number of balloons in each group is $8 \div 4 = m$.
Total number ÷ number of groups
= number in each group
$8 \div 4 = 2$

Each clown is holding 2 balloons.

14. WR

The unknown in this problem is how many markers were in each package.

Example equations:
$72 \div 3 = R$ or $R = 72 \div 3$
$72 \div R = 3$ or $3 = 72 \div R$
$3 \times R = 72$ or $72 = 3 \times R$
$R \times 3 = 72$ or $72 = R \times 3$

No matter which of these related facts you use, the letter R still represents the number of markers in each package, which is 24.

15. **C**

The letter *P* represents the number 12.

To solve this addition problem, you can use the inverse operation of subtraction.

$6 + P = 18$
$18 - 6 = P$
$18 - 6 = 12$
$P = 12$
$6 + 12 = 18$

16. **C**

The number that the letter *A* represents in the given equation is 35.

You can solve this problem by using the inverse operation of subtraction.

$A + 6 = 41$
$A = 41 - 6$
$A = 35$

To check your answer replace *A* with 35.

$35 + 6 = 41$
$41 = 41$

17. **B**

Ava read 7 pages every evening.

The related fact to $56 \div Z = 8$ is $56 \div 8 = Z$.

Since $56 \div 8 = 7$, then $56 \div 7 = 8$.

18. **A**

In the equation $45 = N + 27$, the letter *N* represents the number 18.

Use the inverse operation of subtraction to find the value of *N*.

$45 = N + 27$
$45 - 27 = N$
$45 - 27 = 18$
$N = 18$
$45 = 18 + 27$

Shape and Space

SHAPE AND SPACE

Table of Correlations			
Outcome	Practice Questions	Unit Test Questions	Practice Test
4SS1.0 Use direct and indirect measurement to solve problems			
4SS1.1 *Read and record time, using digital and analog clocks, including 24-hour clocks.*	1, 2, 3, 4, 5	1, 2, 3, 4	28, 29
4SS1.2 *Read and record calendar dates in a variety of formats.*	6, 7	5	30
4SS1.3 *Demonstrate an understanding of area of regular and irregular 2-D shapes.*	8, 9, 10, 11, 12	6, 7, 8, 9	31
4SP2.0 Describe the characteristics of 3-D objects and 2-D shapes, and analyze the relationships among them			
4SS2.4 *Describe and construct right rectangular and right triangular prisms.*	13, 14, 15	10, 11, 12	32, 33
4SS3.0 Describe and analyze position and motion of objects and shapes			
4SS3.5 *Demonstrate an understanding of congruency, concretely and pictorially.*	16, 17, 18	13, 14	34
4SS3.6 *Demonstrate an understanding of line symmetry.*	19, 20, 21, 22	15, 16, 17, 18	35, 36

4SS1.1 *Read and record time, using digital and analog clocks, including 24-hour clocks.*

READING AND RECORDING TIME

Time can be measured in hours, minutes, and seconds.

The following chart shows some time relationships.

24 hours = 1 day
60 minutes = 1 hour
60 seconds = 1 minute

The first 12 hours from midnight to noon is called A.M. (*anti meridian*, which means "before noon"). For example, if you ate breakfast at eight o'clock in the morning, you would write the time as 8:00 A.M.

The next 12 hours from noon to midnight is called P.M. (*post meridian*, which means "after noon"). For example, if you took a bath at eight o'clock in the evening, you would write the time as 8:00 P.M.

12 hours A.M.+ 12 hours P.M.= 24 hours in a day

USING DIGITAL CLOCKS

A **digital clock** shows time using only numerals. Two dots (:) separate the hours from the minutes.

When you read the time on a digital clock, read the number on the left first. The number on the left tells you the hour. Then, read the number to the right of the dots (:). These numbers tell you how many minutes are after the hour.

☼Example

What time is shown on this digital clock?

The clock shows the time of one fifty or "fifty minutes after one."

The number 1 represents the hour. The number 50 represents the number of minutes after the hour.

You can also say that the clock shows the time of "ten minutes to two," which is "10 minutes before 2 o'clock."

USING 12-HOUR ANALOG CLOCKS

An **analog clock** shows time with two hands. The short hand points to the hour and the long hand points to the minutes before or after the hour.

Each line around the circular edge of the clock represents one minute. Each of the twelve numbers on an analog clock represents 1 hour. The hour hand goes around the clock two times to show 24 hours.

To read the time on an analog clock, say the hour first, then the minutes after the hour. For example, 8:32, which means "thirty-two minutes after 8 o'clock."

Example

What time is shown on this analog clock?

The clock shows the time of 9:20.

This time can be written in words as "twenty minutes after nine."

You can also say that the clock shows the time of "forty minutes before ten."

RELATING DIGITAL AND 12-HOUR ANALOG CLOCKS

Time on an analog clock and time on a digital clock is written the same way.

The hour is written first, then two dots (:), then the number of minutes after the hour.

The minutes must always have two digits. For 1 minute to 9 minutes, place a zero before the digits 1 to 9. For example, three minutes after four o'clock would be recorded as 4:03.

The following digital and analog clocks both show the time of 5:20, "twenty minutes after five."

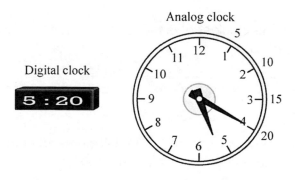

Using 24-Hour Clocks

The 12-hour clock and the 24-hour clock are alike in the way time is read for the first 12 hours of the day (from midnight to noon).

The difference is that you do not use A.M. when reading or writing time using 24-hour clocks. For example, if you ate breakfast at eight in the morning, this is how you would record the time:

- Using a 12-hour clock: I ate breakfast at 8:00 A.M.
- Using a 24-hour clock: I ate breakfast at 08:00.

The main difference between a 12-hour clock and a 24-hour clock is the way time is recorded in the next 12 hours (from noon to midnight).

When the hour hand goes around the clock the second time, the hours continue as 13, 14, 15… up to 24, instead of repeating the numbers 1, 2, 3,…12.

To change the time from 12-hour clock notation to 24-hour clock notation, add 12 to the P.M. hours. The number of minutes will stay the same.

Example

Jan practises the piano at 6:15 P.M. (12-hour notation)

The equivalent time in 24-hour notation is 18:15 (6 + 12 = 18).
6:15 P.M. = 18:15

To change the time from 24-hour clock notation to 12-hour clock notation, subtract 12 from the hours. The minutes will stay the same in both notations.

Example

Ryan walks the dog at 17:45 (24-hour notation).

The equivalent time in 12-hour notation is 5:45 P.M. (17–12 = 5).
17:45 = 5:45 P.M.

Use the following information to answer the next question.

Stefanie and Shawn went skating at 10:25 A.M.

1. Which of the following clocks shows the time that Stefanie and Shawn went skating?

A.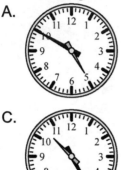

B.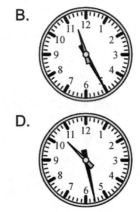

C.

D.

2. An event that would occur during the A.M. is

A. the sun rising   B. the sun setting

C. getting ready to go to bed   D. having an after-school snack

The time shown on this 12-hour clock is 8:32 P.M.

3. On a 24-hour clock, the same time would be written as
   A. 20:32   B. 21:32

   C. 20:32 P.M.   D. 21:32 P.M.

Use the following information to answer the next question.

4. The time shown on the given digital clock is
   A. 8 minutes after 10:00   B. 10 minutes after 8:00

   C. 8 minutes before 10:00   D. 10 minutes before 8:00

Use the following information to answer the next question.

This clock shows the time of 4:00. Will moves the hands on the clock to show a different time.

- He moves the hour hand between the numbers 6 and 7.
- He moves the minute hand to the number 1.

| Written Response |

5. What time will the clock now show?

4SS1.2 *Read and record calendar dates in a variety of formats.*

READING AND RECORDING CALENDAR DATES

Calendars are charts that show the months of the year, what year it is, the days of each week, and the dates of all the days. Here is an example of a calendar page.

May 2007						
S	M	T	W	T	F	S
	1	2	3	4	5	6
7	8	9	10	11	12	(13)
14	15	16	17	18	19	20
21	22	23	24	25	26	27
28	29	30	31			

USING WORDS

When you write a calendar date in words, you usually start with the month, followed by the date, and then the year. A comma is used to separate the date from the year.

For example, the date shown on the calendar page above would be written as May 13, 2007.

USING SYMBOLS

When you write a calendar date using symbols (numbers), a different method is used. The months are represented by the numbers 1 to 12, in order from January to December.

01 January	05 May	09 September
02 February	06 June	10 October
03 March	07 July	11 November
04 April	08 August	12 December

The days are represented by the dates of the days on the calendar. The years are represented by their last two digits.

Each of the three parts must have two digits, so zeros are placed in front of the digits that represent the months and days that only have one digit. A slash (/) is often used to separate the three parts.

Example

One way to record the date is to start with the year, then the month, and then the day.

year / month / day
↓   ↓   ↓
07 / 05 / 13

Another way to record the same date is to start with the day, then the month, and then the year; the reverse order of the example shown above.

day / month / year
↓   ↓   ↓
13 / 05 / 07

6. Raj read the date 28/05/05 on a receipt his mother got when she went shopping. The month the receipt shows is
   A. April
   B. May
   C. June
   D. July

Use the following information to answer the next question.

Marina is excited because she is going to visit her grandmother on the circled date shown on this calendar page.

July 2007						
S	M	T	W	T	F	S
1	2	3	4	5	6	7
8	9	10	11	12	13	14
15	16	17	18	19	20	21
22	(23)	24	25	26	27	28
29	30	31				

7. The circled calendar date can be written as
   A. 06/23/07
   B. 23/07/08
   C. 07/07/23
   D. 23/08/08

4SS1.3 *Demonstrate an understanding of area of regular and irregular 2-D shapes.*

AREA OF REGULAR AND IRREGULAR 2-D SHAPES

Area is the amount of surface that a shape covers. In regular and irregular **2-D shapes** or figures, area is the space inside the lines.

USING SQUARE UNITS

Area is measured in **square units**. For example, the surface of this rectangle is covered with same-size squares.

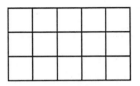

The following methods can be used to find the area of the given rectangle:

- Count the number of squares that cover the surface:
  1, 2, 3, 4…15 sq. units
- Add the number of squares in each row:
  5 + 5 + 5 = 15 sq. units
- Multiply the number of squares in each row by the number of rows:
  5 × 3 = 15 sq. units

USING REFERENTS

To use a **referent** for cm^2 or m^2 means to find an object that has about the same size as a square centimetre or square metre. You can then use that object to help you determine the area of different shapes.

For example, the faces of this die are about 1 cm long on all the sides.

To help you determine the area of a shape in cm^2, you can cover the surface of the shape with dice or you can trace around the edges of a die until the surface of the shape is covered. You would then count the number of dice used or squares drawn to cover the surface to find the area.

ESTIMATING AREA

When estimating area, you are looking for an "about answer." You can use a referent to help you decide what the area could be.

Example

If the shaded square represents 1 m², what would be a good estimate of the area of the given diagram?

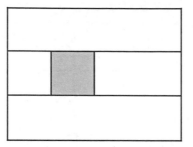

Using the size of the shaded 1 m² square, you can estimate that 4 squares could cover one row.

Since there are 3 rows, you can multiply 4 squares by 3 rows to estimate the area of the given diagram.

$4 \times 3 = 12$ m²

DETERMINING AREA OF IRREGULAR SHAPES

In the following figure, each square represents 1 square centimetre. To find the area of the shaded shape, you need to remember that two half squares equal one full square.

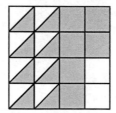

One way to determine the area is to first count the number of shaded squares:
1, 2, 3, 4, 5, 6

Then count every two half-squares as one square:
1, 2, 3, 4

Add the two totals together:
6 + 4 = 10 sq. units

DIFFERENT RECTANGLES WITH SAME AREAS

Rectangles do not need to be **congruent** to have the same area.

:Example

There are four rectangles drawn on the following grid paper.

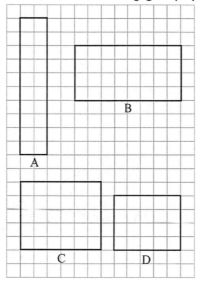

Two of the rectangles have the same area. If each square represents 1 cm^2, which two rectangles have the same area?

Rectangles A and D both have an area of 20 cm^2.

- Rectangle A: $2 \times 10 = 20$ cm^2
- Rectangle D: $5 \times 4 = 20$ c m^2

---

8.   When estimating area, which of the following referents can be used to represent 1 cm^2?

A. Calculator

B. Sugar cube

C. Cereal box

D. Sheet of paper

Use the following information to answer the next question.

Reg uses a referent to estimate the area of the given shape.

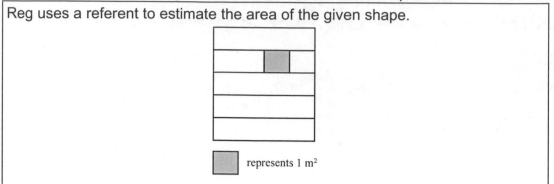

represents 1 m²

9. If the given shaded square represents 1 m², then the **best** estimate of the area of the shape is

A. 15 m²   B. 16 m²

C. 18 m²   D. 20 m²

10. If ☐ represents 1 cm², then which of the following shaded shapes has an area of 8 cm²?

A.

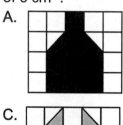

B.

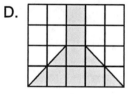

C.

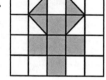

D.

Written Response

11. On the grid shown, draw 2 distinct rectangles that both have an area of 8 square units.

Use only whole numbers for the lengths and widths of the rectangles.
Label the lengths and widths of the rectangles.

For the purposes of this question, two rectangles are not considered distinct if one is simply a rotation of the other.

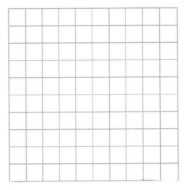

Use the following information to answer the next question.

Bill drew and shaded the following figure on a sheet of graph paper.

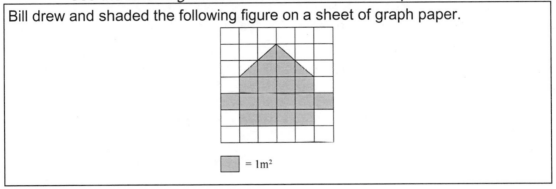

☐ = 1m²

Numerical Response

12. The area of the figure Bill drew and shaded is _____ m².

4SS2.4 *Describe and construct right rectangular and right triangular prisms.*

DESCRIBING PRISMS

You can describe prisms by referring to their faces, edges, and vertices.

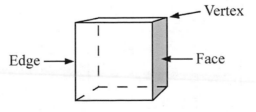

- A **face** is a flat surface on a prism. A face is described by using the name of its 2-D shape, like *triangle*, *square*, or *rectangle*.
- An **edge** is where two faces join together.
- A **vertex** is where the edges meet together to form corners or points.

All **prisms** have rectangular faces. All prisms have two opposite end faces that are **congruent** (the same shape and size). These faces are often called bases and give the prisms their names.

Following are three examples of prisms. One is a **right triangular prism**, and two are **right rectangular prisms**. Right rectangular prisms are often referred to by their names; for example, *cube* or *rectangular prism*.

The opposite end faces (bases) are shaded to help you see how these faces name the prisms.

Right triangular   Cube   Rectangular
prism   (square prism)   prism

Right Rectangular Prisms

All rectangular prisms have 6 faces, 12 edges, and 8 vertices.
Sometimes, the 6 faces are described as 4 sides or lateral faces and 2 bases, top and bottom.

Remember that a cube (square-based prism) is a special kind of rectangular prism. It is made from 6 congruent squares. Cubes also have 6 faces, 12 edges, and 8 vertices.

Name of Prism	Faces	Edges	Vertices	Shape of Base
Rectangular prism	6	12	8	Rectangle
Square prism (cube)	6	12	8	Square

A **net** of a right rectangular prism is a two-dimensional pattern that shows all six faces of the prism. If you fold the net on the lines, you can construct a right rectangular prism.

The net will always have four faces, with one face below the other, as shown below.

The net will also have two other congruent faces (bases), one on each side of the row of four faces. These two faces do not need to be opposite each other in the net, just on each side of the four faces. In the diagrams shown, the bases are shaded.

Both of the following nets will fold into the same right rectangular prism.

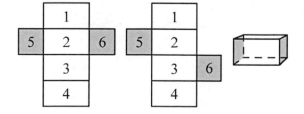

RIGHT TRIANGULAR PRISMS

All triangular prisms have 5 faces, 9 edges, and 6 vertices. Right triangular prisms have two congruent right-angled triangles (the same size and shape) at opposite ends of the prism. The other three faces are rectangles.

Name of Prism	Faces	Edges	Vertices	Shape of Base
Triangular prism	5	9	6	Triangle

A **net** of a right triangular prism is a two-dimensional pattern that shows all five faces of the prism. If you fold the net on the lines, you can construct a triangular prism.

The net will always have three rectangular faces. The two right-angled triangular faces will be on opposite sides of the rectangles. Following is one example of a net for a right triangular prism.

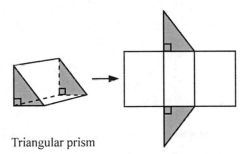

Triangular prism

Use the following information to answer the next question.

Lisa uses straws and marshmallows to make a model of a right rectangular prism.

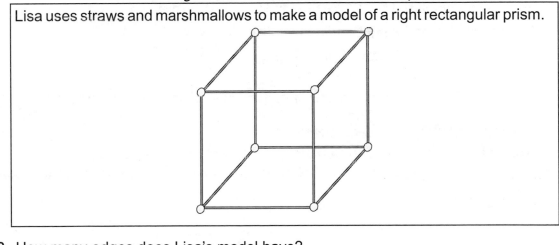

13. How many edges does Lisa's model have?

    A. 6   B. 8

    C. 12   D. 14

14. Which of the following nets can be folded on the lines to make a right rectangular prism?

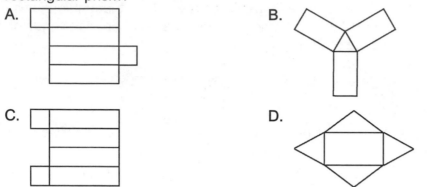

A.

B.

C.

D.

Use the following information to answer the next question.

Jeff plans to use pattern blocks to make a model of this right triangular prism.

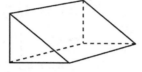

15. To make a model of the right triangular prism, Jeff needs

A. 2 rectangles and 3 right angle triangles

B. 3 rectangles and 3 right angle triangles

C. 2 rectangles and 2 right angle triangles

D. 3 rectangles and 2 right angle triangles

4SS3.5 *Demonstrate an understanding of congruency, concretely and pictorially.*

IDENTIFYING CONGRUENT 2-D SHAPES

When shapes are said to be **congruent**, they are the same size and shape.

For example, the two triangles shown below are the same size and shape, so they are congruent triangles.

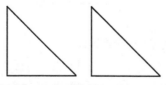

Shapes can be in different positions and still be congruent. For example, the three triangles shown below are in different positions, but they are still congruent because they all have the same shape and size.

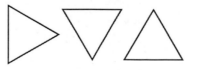

Example

Gino has the given triangle pattern block on his desk.

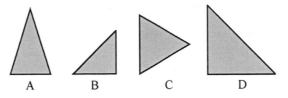

Which of these triangle pattern blocks is congruent to Gino's triangle pattern block?

A   B   C   D

To answer this question, look for a triangle that has the same shape as Gino's triangle. It must also be the same size as Gino's triangle.

Triangles B and D look to be the same shape as Gino's triangle, but only triangle D is the same shape and size as Gino's triangle.

Triangle D is congruent to Gino's triangle even though it is in a different position.

Use the following information to answer the next question.

When Maddie places these pattern blocks in a row, she sees that two of the blocks have congruent shapes.

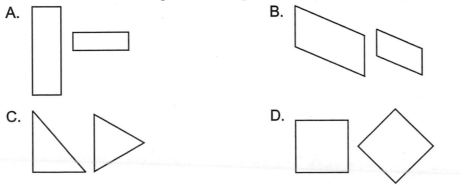

16. The two blocks that are congruent are
    A. Blocks A and E
    B. Blocks B and D
    C. Blocks C and F
    D. Blocks F and G

17. In which of the following sets of diagrams are there two congruent shapes?

A.

B.

C.

D.

18. In which of the following sets are the triangles congruent?

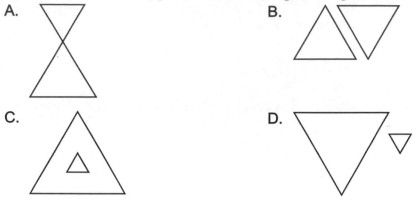

4SS3.6 *Demonstrate an understanding of line symmetry.*

SYMMETRICAL SHAPES

A 2-D shape has symmetry when half of the shape looks exactly like the other half.

You can think of a **line of symmetry** as a fold line. When a shape is folded in half along a line of symmetry, both sides are exactly the same. That means that the shape is symmetrical.

Shapes can be made symmetrical by horizontal, vertical, or diagonal lines of symmetry. The following diagrams show symmetrical shapes using these different lines.

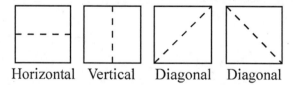

Horizontal　Vertical　Diagonal　Diagonal

LINES OF SYMMETRY

Some shapes do not have a line of symmetry, some shapes have only one line of symmetry, and some shapes have more than one line of symmetry.

The following 2-D shapes are sorted according to the number of lines of symmetry they each have.

- No lines of symmetry:

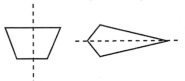

- One line of symmetry:

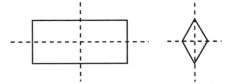

- Two lines of symmetry:

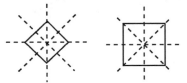

- More than two lines of symmetry:

Use the following information to answer the next question.

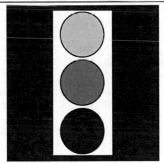

Walking home from school, Layla stopped to look at the traffic lights near her house.

19. How many lines of symmetry does the picture of the traffic lights have?

   A. 0   B. 1

   C. 2   D. 4

20. Which of the following shapes has one line of symmetry?

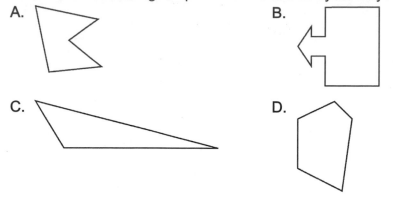

A.

B.

C.

D.

Use the following information to answer the next question.

When Aisha went to the fruit market, she noticed that some pieces of fruit were so evenly formed that they could have a line of symmetry. When she got home, she drew a picture of an apple, a mango, a banana, and a pineapple.

21. On which of the following pictures could Aisha **best** draw a line of symmetry?

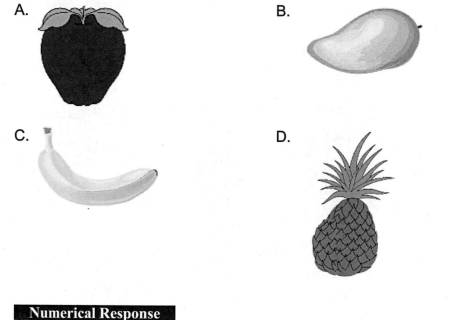

A.

B.

C.

D.

Numerical Response

22. How many lines of symmetry does a square have? _____

ANSWERS AND SOLUTIONS
SHAPE AND SPACE

1. C	6. B	11. WR	16. C	21. A
2. A	7. C	12. 18	17. D	22. 4
3. A	8. B	13. C	18. B	
4. B	9. D	14. A	19. B	
5. WR	10. D	15. D	20. B	

1. C

This clock shows the time of 10:25.

To show 10:25, the hour hand must point between 10 and 11, and the minute hand must point to 5.

2. A

The sun rising would occur during the A.M.

3. A

On a 24-hour clock, the same time would be written as 20:32.

When changing time from a 12-hour clock to a 24-hour clock, add 12 hours to the P.M. hours: 8 + 12 = 20

The minutes will stay the same.
8:32 P.M.= 20:32

4. B

The time shown is 10 minutes after 8:00.

The number to the left of the two dots (:) tells you the hour. This clock tells you that the hour is 8:00.

The two digits to the right of the two dots (:) tell you how many minutes are after the hour. This clock tells you that there are 10 minutes after the hour.

5. WR

When the hour hand (short hand) points between 6 and 7, the hour is 6:00, so the number 6 is written to the left of the two dots. 6:_____

When the minute hand (long hand) points to the 1, it is in the 5-minute position: 5 minutes after 6 o'clock.

Remember to place a 0 in front of the 5 for the 5-minute position.

The clock will now show 6:05.

6. B

The fifth month of the year is May, and it is represented by the number 05.
January, February, March, April, May

7. C

July 23, 2007, can be represented as 07/07/23: year, month, day.

The year is 2007, so the year is represented by the number 07.

July is the 7th month of the year, so the month is represented by the number 07.

The day is the 23rd, so the day is represented by the number 23.

8. B

A sugar cube is the best referent for 1 cm². All 4 sides on all 6 faces of the cube are about 1 cm long.

9. D

The best estimate of the area of the shape is 20 m².

It looks like 4 squares would fit side by side in the second row, 2 to the left of the given square and 1 to the right of the given square.

Since there are 5 rows in all, you can multiply 4 by 5 to get an estimated area. $4 \times 5 = 20$ m²

10. D

This shape has an area of 8 cm².

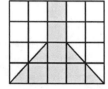

There are 6 full squares and 4 half squares. The 4 half squares are equal to 2 full squares.
$6 + 2 = 8$

11. WR

Example rectangles

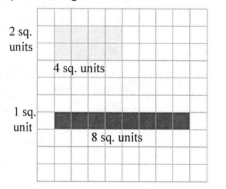

2 sq. units

4 sq. units

1 sq. unit

8 sq. units

The top rectangle has an area of 8 sq. units. $2 \times 4 = 8$ sq. units

The bottom rectangle also has an area of 8 sq. units. $1 \times 8 = 8$ sq. units

12. 18

Count the number of shaded squares: 1, 2, 3, ...16 m².

Count every two shaded half-squares as one square: 1, 2 m²

Add the two totals: $16 + 2 = 18$ m²

13. C

Lisa's model has 12 edges.

An edge is where two faces meet on a 3-D object. In Lisa's model, each straw represents one edge.

There are 4 edges at the bottom, around the base.

There are 4 edges at the top, around the top face.

There are 4 vertical edges on the sides.
$4 + 4 + 4 = 12$

14. A

This net will fold into a right rectangular prism.

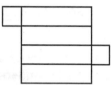

Nets for rectangular prisms have four rectangles in a row.
There are also two congruent rectangles, one on each side of the row of four.

15. D

To make the model, Jeff needs 3 rectangles and 2 right angle triangles.

All triangular prisms have three rectangular faces and two triangular bases.

16. C

Blocks C and F are congruent because they both have the same shape and size.

17. D

This set of diagrams has two congruent shapes.

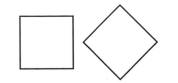

The two squares are congruent because they have the same shape and size, even though they are in a different position.

18. B

The triangles in this set are congruent.

The two triangles have the same size and shape; they are just in different positions.

19. B

There is only 1 line of symmetry in this picture of traffic lights.

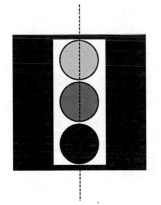

Remember that the two halves of the picture, when folded on the line of symmetry, must be identical in size and shape. Because this picture has different shades of colour for the three traffic lights, the two halves must also be identical in colour.

20. B

This shape has one line of symmetry.

It is the only shape that can be folded in half, with the two parts being exactly the same size and shape.

21. A

The picture of the apple is the most likely piece of fruit to have a line of symmetry drawn through it, with the two halves matching exactly.

22. 4

A square has 4 lines of symmetry:
One is vertical (line 1).
One is horizontal (line 3).
Two are diagonal (lines 2 and 4).

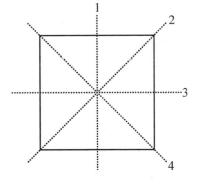

UNIT TEST

Use the following information to answer the next question.

On Friday night, Paulo and his family were watching a movie. The movie ended at the time shown on the given clock.

1. The movie ended at
   A. 5:50 A.M.
   B. 5:50 P.M.
   C. 10:25 A.M.
   D. 10:25 P.M.

2. Which of the following events can happen in both the A.M. and P.M.?
   A. Reading before bedtime
   B. Eating supper after school
   C. Taking the school bus
   D. Watching fireworks in the night sky.

Use the following information to answer the next question.

This 12-hour clock shows a time of 4:35 in the morning.

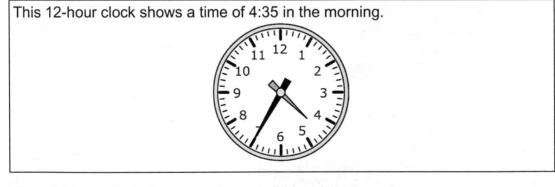

3. On a 24-hour clock, the same time would be shown as
   A. 04:35
   B. 07:22
   C. 14:35
   D. 16:35

Use the following information to answer the next question.

This analog clock shows the time when Mary's dance lessons begin.

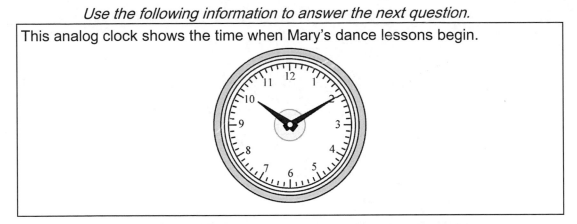

4. The digital clock that shows the time Mary's dance lessons begin is

A.

2:10

B.

2:50

C.

10:02

D.

10:10

5. The zoo was closed on 10/11/08. Which calendar page shows this date?

A.

September 2008						
S	M	T	W	T	F	S
		1	2	3	4	5
6	7	8	9	10	(11)	12
13	14	15	16	17	18	19
20	21	22	23	24	25	26
27	28	29	30			

B.

October 2008						
S	M	T	W	T	F	S
				1	2	3
4	5	6	7	8	9	(10)
11	12	13	14	15	16	17
18	19	20	21	22	23	24
25	26	27	28	29	30	31

C.

November 2008						
S	M	T	W	T	F	S
1	2	3	4	5	6	7
8	9	(10)	11	12	13	14
15	16	17	18	19	20	21
22	23	24	25	26	27	28
29	30					

D.

December 2008						
S	M	T	W	T	F	S
		1	2	3	4	5
6	7	8	9	10	(11)	12
13	14	15	16	17	18	19
20	21	22	23	24	25	26
27	28	29	30	31		

Use the following information to answer the next question.

Leslie drew the following design on grid paper.

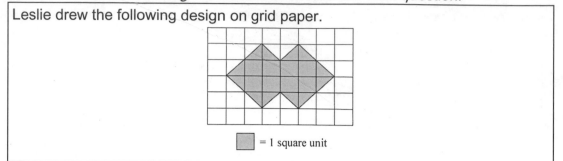

= 1 square unit

6. The area of the design Leslie drew is
   A. 48 square units
   B. 34 square units
   C. 20 square units
   D. 14 square units

Use the following information to answer the next question.

Kelly coloured four words on squared papers. Each square represents 1 sq. unit.

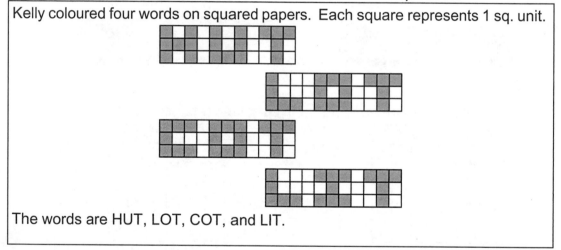

The words are HUT, LOT, COT, and LIT.

7. Listed in order from greatest area to least area, the words are
   A. COT, HUT, LOT, LIT
   B. LIT, LOT, HUT, COT
   C. COT, HUT, LIT, LOT
   D. LOT, LIT, HUT, COT

Use the following information to answer the next question.

Kim makes four shapes out of square blocks.

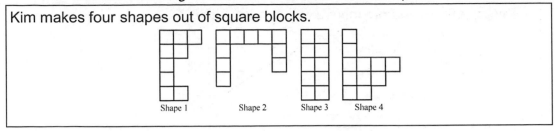

Shape 1   Shape 2   Shape 3   Shape 4

8. If each square block represents 1 square unit, the two shapes that both have an area of 10 square units are

A. shapes 1 and 2

B. shapes 2 and 3

C. shapes 2 and 4

D. shapes 3 and 4

Use the following information to answer the next question.

Ken draws a triangle, a pentagon, and a square on squared grid paper.

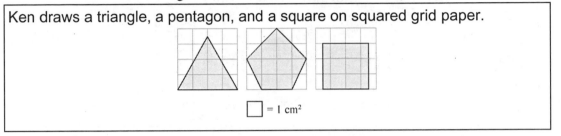

☐ = 1 cm²

Written Response

9. Estimate the area of each shape to the nearest whole centimetre.

Explain your work.

10. The name of a prism is determined by the

A. shape of its base

B. shape of its side faces

C. number of faces it has

D. number of edges it has

Use the following information to answer the next question.

The figure shown is a model of a rectangular prism.

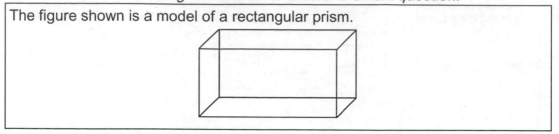

11. All rectangular prisms have

    A. 4 faces and 6 vertices   B. 4 faces and 10 vertices

    C. 6 faces and 8 vertices   D. 6 faces and 12 vertices

Use the following information to answer the next question.

Jenny plans to fold these nets into right rectangular prisms.

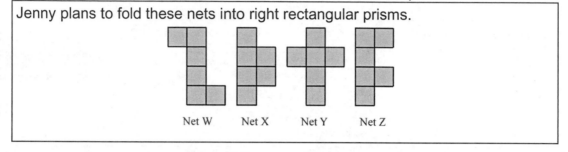

            Net W   Net X   Net Y   Net Z

12. Which two nets will Jenny **not** be able to fold into rectangular prisms?

    A. Nets W and X   B. Nets W and Z

    C. Nets X and Y   D. Nets X and Z

Use the following information to answer the next question.

Miss Wilson asked her students to draw and colour a design that showed at least one pair of congruent shapes.
This is the design that Sato made.

13. How many pairs of congruent shapes are in Sato's design?

    A. 1 pair   B. 2 pairs

    C. 3 pairs   D. 4 pairs

14. The shapes in which of the following sets are congruent?

A.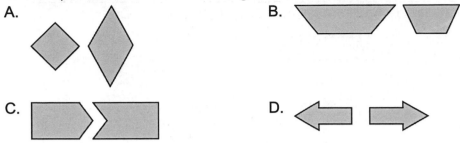

B.

C.

D.

Use the following information to answer the next question.

When Kyra was asked to draw lines of symmetry through four shapes, she drew 2 lines through every shape.

15. In which of the following shapes did Kyra correctly draw 2 lines of symmetry?

A.

B.

C.

D.

16. The picture that correctly shows a line of symmetry is

A.

B.

C.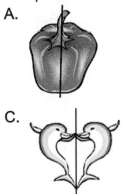

D.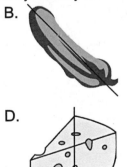

Use the following information to answer the next question.

Zoe draws one line through the middle of four different shapes.

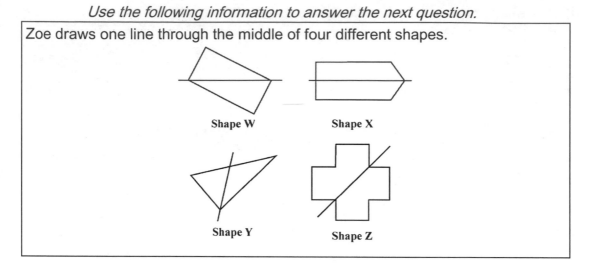

Shape W   Shape X

Shape Y   Shape Z

17. The two shapes that each have a line of symmetry are

   A. shapes W and X   B. shapes W and Y

   C. shapes X and Y   D. shapes X and Z

Use the following information to answer the next question.

Carla sees this symmetrical shape on the side of a van in a parking lot.

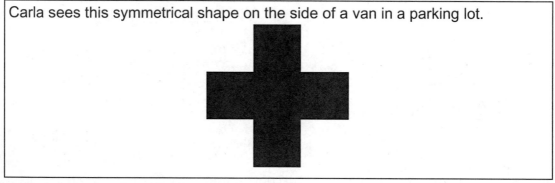

Numerical Response

18. How many lines of symmetry does the given shape have?_____

ANSWERS AND SOLUTIONS – UNIT TEST

1.	D	6.	D	11.	C	16.	C
2.	C	7.	A	12.	D	17.	D
3.	A	8.	B	13.	D	18.	4
4.	D	9.	WR	14.	D		
5.	C	10.	A	15.	D		

1. D

The movie ended at 10:25 P.M.

The hour hand points between 10 and 11, so it is after 10 o'clock.

The minute hand points to the 5, which is the 25-minute position (5, 10, 15, 20, 25).

The family is watching the movie on Friday night, so the time is written with P.M.

2. C

You can take the school bus to school in the morning (A.M.) and take the bus home in the afternoon (P.M.)

3. A

On a 24-hour clock, the same time would be shown as 04:35.

The time would look the same as the time on a 12-hour clock, except that you would not write A.M. after the time.

4. D

This digital clock shows the time Mary's dance lessons begin:

The hour hand on the analog clock points between the 10 and 11. That means that it is after 10 o'clock.

The minute hand on the analog clock points to the number 2, which is the 10-minute position.
The time is ten minutes after ten o'clock.

5. C

This calendar page shows the date 10/11/08:

November 2008						
S	M	T	W	T	F	S
1	2	3	4	5	6	7
8	9	⑩	11	12	13	14
15	16	17	18	19	20	21
22	23	24	25	26	27	28
29	30					

1st number: The circled number is the tenth day of the month and is represented by the number 10.

2nd number: November is the eleventh month of the year and is represented by the number 11.

3rd number: The year is 2008 and is represented by the number 08.

6. D

The area of the design Leslie drew is 14 square units.

Count the number of full squares in the design: 1, 2, 3, ...8 square units

Count every 2 half-squares as one square: 1, 2, 3, 4, 5, 6 square units

Add the two totals: 8 + 6 = 14 square units

7. A

From greatest area to least area, the words are COT, HUT, LOT, LIT.

Count the total number of shaded squares of each of the three letters that make up each word.

Area of COT: 20 sq. units

Area of HUT: 19 sq. units

Area of LOT: 18 sq. units

Area of LIT: 17 sq. units

8. B

Shapes 2 and 3 both have an area of 10 square units.

9. WR

Example explanations

Triangle

I counted 2 whole squares and 2 almost whole squares. 2 + 2 = 4

I counted the two part squares on the left and on the right as 2 whole squares.

I counted the two half squares at the top as 1 whole square.

I added the totals to get an estimated area. $4 + 2 + 1 = 7$ c m^2

Pentagon

I counted 6 whole squares.

I counted the four half squares as 2 whole squares.

I counted the two part squares on the bottom left and bottom right as 2 whole squares.

I added the totals to get an estimated area. $6 + 2 + 2 = 10$ c m^2

Square

I counted 6 whole squares.

I counted the six half squares as 3 whole squares.

I added the totals to get an estimated area. $6 + 3 = 9$ cm^2

10. A

The name of a prism is determined by the shape of its base.

All right rectangular prisms have right-angled rectangular bases.

All right triangular prisms have right-angled triangular bases.

11. C

All rectangular prisms have 6 faces and 8 vertices.

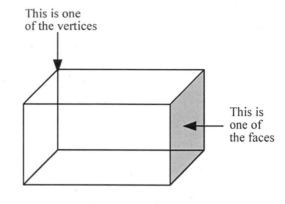

This is one of the vertices

This is one of the faces

12. D

Nets X and Z will **not** fold into rectangular prisms.

Nets for rectangular prisms must have one face on each side of the row of four faces. Nets X and Z have the two faces on the same side of the row.

13. D

There are 4 pairs of congruent shapes in Sato's design.

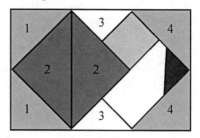

Remember: There are two parts to a pair. That means the two shapes numbered 1 make one pair, and the two shapes numbered 4 make another pair, even though all four of the shapes are congruent.

14. **D**

> The shapes in this set are congruent.

> The two arrows are exactly the same size and shape. The only difference between the arrows is that they are flipped in different directions.

15. **D**

> Kyra correctly drew 2 lines of symmetry in this shape.

> If you folded the shape along each line of symmetry, the two pieces would fit over each other exactly.

16. **C**

> This picture correctly shows a line of symmetry.

> The two sides of the line of symmetry are identical. They are mirror images of each other.

17. **D**

> Shapes X and Z both have a line of symmetry.
>
> When you fold a shape on its line of symmetry, the two parts will fit over each other exactly, having the same size and shape.

18. **4**

> The given shape has 1 vertical, 1 horizontal, and 2 diagonal lines of symmetry (just like a square does).

NOTES

STATISTICS AND PROBABILITY (DATA ANALYSIS)

Table of Correlations			
Outcome	Practice Questions	Unit Test Questions	Practice Test
4SP1.0 Collect, display and analyze data to solve problems			
4SP1.1 *Demonstrate an understanding of many-to-one correspondence.*	1, 2, 3	1, 2, 3	37, 38
4SP1.2 *Construct and interpret pictographs and bar graphs involving many-to-one correspondence to draw conclusions.*	4, 5, 6, 7, 8, 9, 10, 11, 12, 13	4, 5, 6, 7, 8, 9, 10, 11	39, 40, 41

4SP1.1 *Demonstrate an understanding of many-to-one correspondence.*

USING MANY-TO-ONE CORRESPONDENCE

Many-to-one correspondence means that each picture, symbol, line, or square in a graph represents more than one item.

When you use many-to-one correspondence instead of one-to-one correspondence in a graph, you are able to represent larger numbers in a smaller space. The graph would be smaller and more manageable, making it easier to read.

For example, if you are making a bar graph that has data in the thousands, make each line or square represent 1 000 instead of 10. Your graph will be smaller, easier to read, and easier to interpret.

IN PICTOGRAPHS

In a **pictograph**, symbols or pictures show the **data**. A **key** shows the number that each symbol or picture represents.

When reading many-to-one correspondence in a pictograph, you need to be careful if only half of a symbol is shown. A half symbol is worth half the value of the whole symbol.

Example

Reading the given pictograph, how many children chose soccer as their favourite summer activity?

Favourite Summer Activities	
Soccer	😊😊◖
Baseball	😊😊😊😊
Swimming	😊😊😊
Biking	😊◖
Hiking	😊😊

Key: 😊 represents 2 children

To solve this problem, count by 2s for the full faces, since each face represents 2 children.

Count the half face as 1 child, since the half face represents half the value of a full face. 2, 4, 5

Five children chose soccer as their favourite activity.

IN BAR GRAPHS

In a **bar graph**, bars show the data. Numbers on an axis show the scale used. Scales are usually on the left side of the graph, on the *y*-axis; however, this is not always the case.

A **scale** shows you what number each line or square represents. On a bar graph, the value of the space between two lines is referred to as an **interval**.

When reading many-to-one correspondence, be careful to check if the bar is shown halfway between two lines. If it is, that would mean that the value of the bar is half of the interval.

Example

What kind of interval is used in the given bar graph?
How many beetles did Eric count?

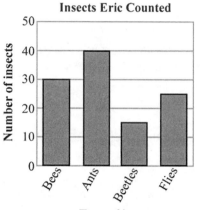

To answer the question about the interval, look at the numbers on the left side of the graph. Each line counts up by 10. That means that the interval is 10. When a bar stops at half a square, like in "Beetles," the value will be half of ten, which is 5.

To answer the question about the number of beetles counted, start at the 0 and count up to where the bar ends.

10, 15 (one interval of 10 and one half-interval of 5)
Eric counted 15 beetles.

_____

Use the following information to answer the next question.

The pictograph below represents the number of stickers Chung collected in one month.

Stickers Chung Collected

Chung

1. If Chung collected 44 stickers in one month, then each face in the pictograph represents

   A. 1 sticker

   B. 2 stickers

   C. 4 stickers

   D. 11 stickers

Use the following information to answer the next question.

This graph shows the number of books that six students read.

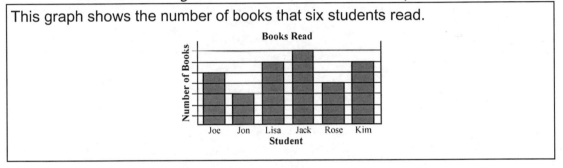

2. If Jack read 21 books, how many books does each line on the graph represent?

   A. 1 book

   B. 2 books

   C. 3 books

   D. 7 books

Use the following information to answer the next question.

The chart below shows the number of students who voted for their favourite type of movie.

Favorite Type of Movie	Number of Students
Action	6
Comedy	12
Drama	8
Horror	4
Mystery	10

Written Response

3. If you were going to draw a pictograph to display this data, what kind of many-to-one correspondence would you use?

   Explain your answer.

4SP1.2 *Construct and interpret pictographs and bar graphs involving many-to-one correspondence to draw conclusions.*

INTERPRETING DATA TO DRAW CONCLUSIONS

When you read graphs, you need to pay close attention to all the data shown. Some information to look for includes the following:

- labels of the axes
- information in the title
- the scales, keys, or intervals used

You can interpret or compare the data you read. Mathematical operations can be made using the data. You can look at all the data and draw conclusions about it.

Example

The following bar graph shows the number of students who chose one of four favourite insects.

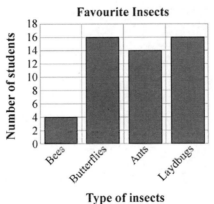

One fact you can learn from reading the bar graph is that 14 students chose ants as their favourite insect.

When you interpret the data in this graph, one fact you can learn is that 12 more students like ladybugs than bees.

$16 - 4 = 12$

A conclusion you can draw from the data shown is that of the four given insects, bees are the least popular.

___

Use the following information to answer the next question.

Gerri recorded the weather every day for the month of June. She recorded her observations in the following chart.

Weather in June

☀	Sunny	12 days
	Windy	3 days
	Cloudy	9 days
	Rainy	6 days

Written Response

4. Create a pictograph showing the same information that is shown in the chart, using many-to-one correspondence.

   Choose a symbol or picture to use in your pictograph to represent a certain number of days.

   Remember to include a key and to make a title for your graph.

This pictograph shows the number of cookies that students in grades 1, 2, 3, and 4 ate at their year-end party.

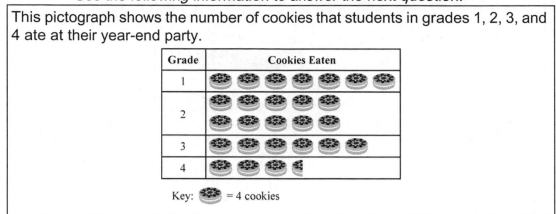

Grade	Cookies Eaten
1	
2	
3	
4	

Key: = 4 cookies

5. How many more cookies did the Grade 2 students eat than the Grade 4 students?

    A. 14   B. 24

    C. 26   D. 36

This bar graph represents the favourite activities for a group of Grade 4 students.

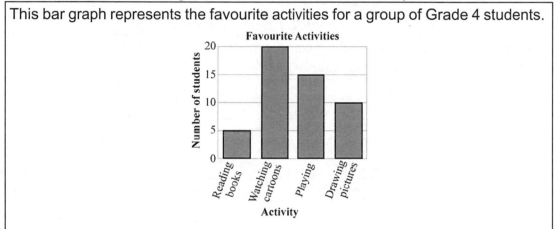

6. How many more students chose watching cartoons and playing than chose reading books and drawing pictures?

    A. 35   B. 25

    C. 20   D. 15

Use the following information to answer the next question.

Mr. French's science students made a bar graph showing their favourite birds.

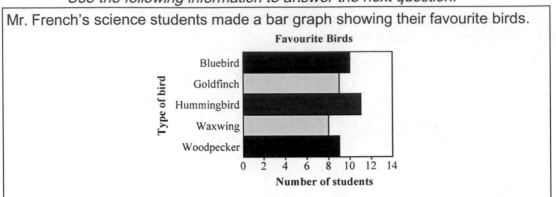

7. What types of birds were chosen by a total of 26 students?

    A. Bluebird, goldfinch, and waxwing

    B. Bluebird, goldfinch, and woodpecker

    C. Goldfinch, waxwing, and woodpecker

    D. Goldfinch, hummingbird, and woodpecker

Use the following information to answer the next question.

Will surveyed his classmates to see how many pets each student has. He displayed the data he collected in a pictograph.

Number of Pets				
1 pet	☺	☺	☺	☺
2 pets	☺	☺	◖	
3 pets	☺	◖		
4 pets	☺			
5 pets	◖			
No pets	☺	☺	☺	

Key: ☺ = 2 students

8. How many of Will's classmates have pets?

    A. 11   B. 19

    C. 22   D. 25

Use the following information to answer the next question.

This pictograph shows the number of children who participate in four different after-school activities.

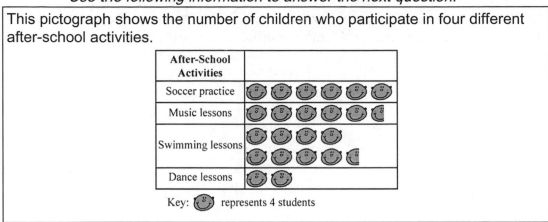

Key: 😊 represents 4 students

9. Which of the following statements about the data is **true**?
    A. There are 12 students who take dance lessons.
    B. There are 36 students who take swimming lessons.
    C. There are 14 more students who take dance lessons than music lessons.
    D. There are 2 more students who go to soccer practise than take music lessons.

Use the following information to answer the next question.

Elva asked some students in her school, "What is your favourite type of music: rock, country, pop, or hip hop?"
Elva used their answers to make the following pictograph.

Favourite Type of Music	Number of Students
Rock	💿💿💿💿💿💿💿💿💿
Country	💿💿💿💿💿
Pop	💿💿💿💿💿💿💿
Hip hop	💿💿💿💿

Key: 💿 represents 5 students

10. Which of the following statements about the information in the pictograph is **not** true?
    A. There are 10 fewer students who chose rock than chose pop.
    B. There are 10 fewer students who chose hip hop than chose pop.
    C. There are 15 more students who chose rock than chose country.
    D. There are 5 more students who chose country than chose hip hop.

Use the following information to answer the next question.

Hudson surveyed students in his school to see which one of six summer sports they liked the most. He made this bar graph to show the data he collected.

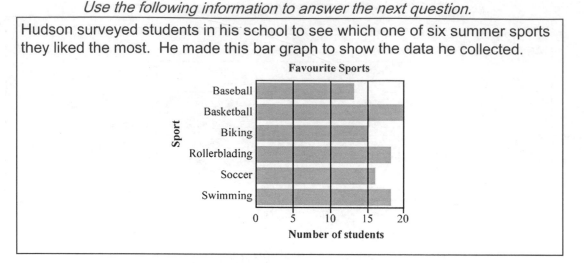

11. Which of the following conclusions can be drawn from the data Hudson collected?

   A. Soccer is the most popular sport.

   B. Baseball is more popular than biking.

   C. Basketball is the least popular sport.

   D. Rollerblading is just as popular as swimming.

Use the following information to answer the next question.

This bar graph represents the population of a town over a period of four years.

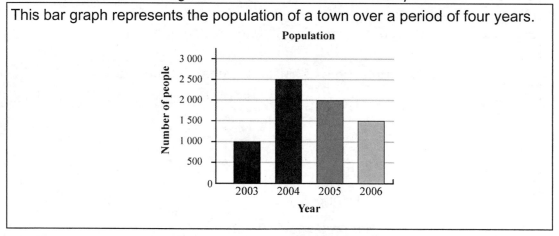

12. The interval used in the given graph is

   A. 5   B. 100

   C. 500   D. 1 000

Use the following information to answer the next question.

This pictograph shows the data collected in a survey in which children were asked to name their favourite flavour of ice cream.

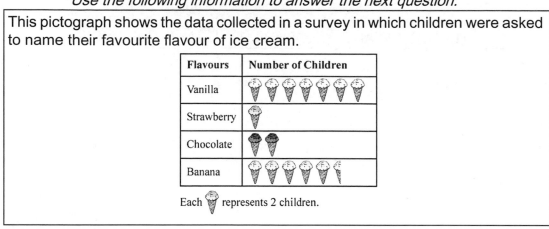

Flavours	Number of Children
Vanilla	🍦🍦🍦🍦🍦🍦🍦
Strawberry	🍦
Chocolate	🍦🍦
Banana	🍦🍦🍦🍦🍦🍦

Each 🍦 represents 2 children.

Numerical Response

13. How many children participated in the survey? _____

ANSWERS AND SOLUTIONS
STATISTICS AND PROBABILITY (DATA ANALYSIS)

1. C	5. C	9. D	13. 31
2. C	6. C	10. A	
3. WR	7. C	11. D	
4. WR	8. B	12. C	

1. C

Each face in the pictograph represents 4 stickers.

There are 11 faces in the pictograph.

There are 11 groups of 4 in the number 44.
11 + 11 + 11 + 11 = 44

2. C

Each line on the graph represents 3 books.

Count the number of spaces or intervals that make up the bar that represents the number of books Jack read. There are 7 intervals.

Since Jack read 21 books, divide 21 by 7.
21 ÷ 7 = 3

The lines on the graph count up by 3s.
3, 6, 9, 12, 15, 18, 21

3. WR

Example correspondence
I would use a key in which 1 face represented 2 students.

Example explanation
I chose 2 for my key because all the numbers in the data set are even numbers.

The numbers can all be divided evenly by 2, so I will not need to use a half face for a half value.

The most number of faces I would need would be 6, so the graph would not be too big.

4. WR

Example graph

Weather in June

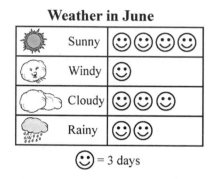

$\bigodot$ = 3 days

5. C

The Grade 2 students ate 26 more cookies than the Grade 4 students.

Grade 2 students: 10 × 4 = 40

Grade 4 students: 3 × 4 = 12

Since a half cookie has half the value of a whole cookie, add 2 to 12 to get the total number of cookies. 12 + 2 = 14

Subtract the two amounts to determine the difference. 40 – 14 = 26

6. C

Twenty more students chose watching cartoons and playing than chose reading books and drawing pictures.

Watching cartoons and playing:
20 + 15 = 35
Reading books and drawing pictures:
5 + 10 = 15

Subtract the two totals to find the difference. 35 – 15 = 20

7. C

A total of 26 students chose goldfinch, waxwing, and woodpecker.

Goldfinch: 9 students
Waxwing: 8 students
Woodpecker: 9 students
9 + 8 + 9 = 26

8. B

A total of 19 classmates have pets.

Be careful when you read the graph. Do not count the 3 faces that represent the number of classmates who do not have any pets.

Example strategy
Each face represents 2 children. Count the number of full faces and multiply by 2. 8 × 2 = 16

Each half face represents 1 classmate (half of two is one).
Count the number of half faces and multiply by 1. 3 × 1 = 3

Add the two totals. 16 + 3 = 19

9. D

The statement that is **true** is: there are 2 more students who go to soccer practise than take music lessons.

Since each face represents 4 students, then a half face represents 2 students.

Soccer practice: 6 × 4 = 24
Music lessons: 5 × 4 = 20 and
20 + 2 = 22

Subtract to find the difference.
24 − 22 = 2

10. A

The statement that is not true is: there are 10 fewer students who chose rock than chose pop.

Since 40 students chose rock (8 × 5 = 40) and 30 students chose pop (6 × 5 = 30), there were 10 more students who chose rock, not 10 fewer.

11. D

The conclusion that can be drawn from the data collected is "rollerblading is just as popular as swimming".

The bars that represent rollerblading and swimming stop at the same place on the graph, between 15 and 20.

Rollerblading and swimming were both chosen by about 18 students.

12. C

The interval used in the given graph is 500.

The graph starts at 0 and then adds 500 to each number to get the next number.

Each line on the graph represents another 500.
0, 500, 500 + 500 = 1 000,
1 000 + 500 = 1 500, …3 000.

13. 31

Since each ice-cream cone represents 2 children, count the cones by 2s.

The half cone will represent half of 2 children, which is 1 child.

Vanilla: 2, 4, 6, 8, 10, 12, 14,
Strawberry: ….16,
Chocolate: ….18, 20,
Banana: ….22, 24, 26, 28, 30, 31

UNIT TEST

Use the following information to answer the next question.

Lucy made a pictograph to show the number of cards she and three friends received on Valentine's Day.

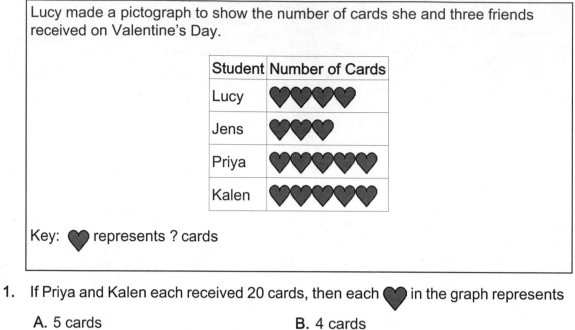

Key: ♥ represents ? cards

1. If Priya and Kalen each received 20 cards, then each ♥ in the graph represents

   A. 5 cards

   C. 3 cards

   B. 4 cards

   D. 2 cards

Shay made a pictograph to display the kinds of exercises students in his class enjoy.

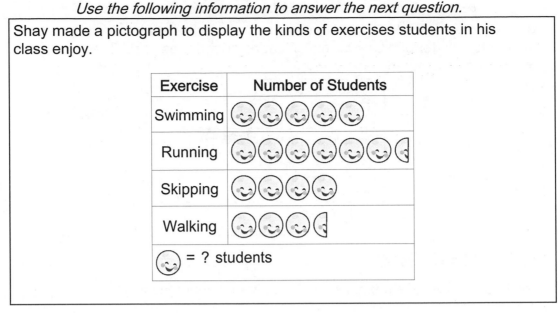

2. If 39 students like running, then each represents

   A. 3 students   B. 4 students

   C. 5 students   D. 6 students

This graph shows the number of books on each shelf in a class library.

Numerical Response

3. If there are 56 books on the 4th shelf, how many books does each represent? _____

Use the following information to answer the next question.

Mrs. Brown and Mrs. Hailes are planning a party for their students. They ask each student to vote for one type of muffin that he or she likes best. The results are shown in the pictograph below.

Banana nut	🧁🧁🧁🧁
Blueberry	🧁🧁🧁
Chocolate chip	🧁🧁🧁🧁🧁
Cranberry	🧁🧁🧁
Oatmeal raisin	🧁🧁🧁🧁

Key: 🧁 = 3 votes

Numerical Response

4. The total number of students who voted for a favourite muffin is _____.

Use the following information to answer the next question.

The following pictograph shows the number of different-coloured cars that a car salesman sold in one month.

Cars Sold

Red   White   Yellow   Blue

Key: 🚗 represents 5 cars

5. The car salesman sold a total of 45
   A. red and white cars
   B. white and blue cars
   C. yellow and blue cars
   D. white and yellow cars

Use the following information to answer the next question.

The following graph shows the heights of six buildings.

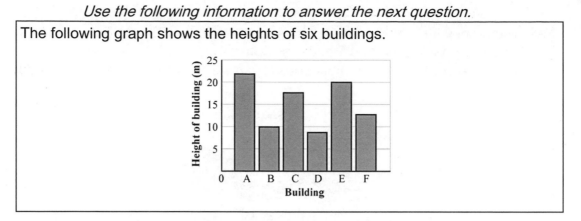

6. The two buildings that are taller than 10 metres and shorter than 20 metres are
   A. buildings B and C
   B. buildings B and E
   C. buildings C and F
   D. buildings E and F

Use the following information to answer the next question.

To raise money for a fundraiser at their school, a group of Grade Four students sold 250 seed packages from Monday to Saturday.

The graph below shows the number of seed packages that were sold from Monday to Friday.

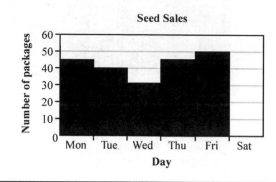

7. The bar that shows the number of seed packages sold on Saturday is

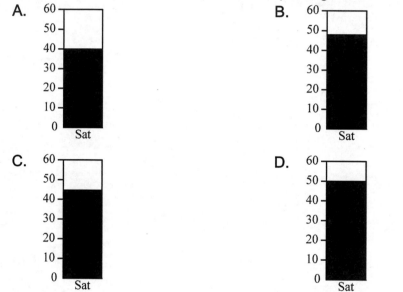

A.

B.

C.

D.

Use the following information to answer the next question.

The following pictograph shows the number of treats sold on a track-and-field day at school.

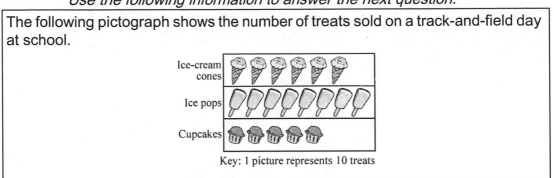

Key: 1 picture represents 10 treats

8. Which of the following statements is **true**?
   A. There were 200 treats sold altogether.
   B. Twice as many ice pops than cupcakes were sold.
   C. There were 10 more ice pops sold than ice-cream cones.
   D. There were 10 fewer cupcakes sold than ice-cream cones.

Use the following information to answer the next question.

This bar graph shows the number of quarters that five children collected.

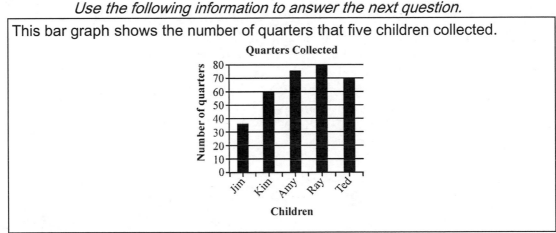

9. Which child collected twice as many quarters as Jim?
   A. Kim   B. Amy
   C. Ray   D. Ted

Use the following information to answer the next question.

This bar graph shows the heights, in centimetres, of four boys: Henry, Joseph, Patrick, and Thomas.

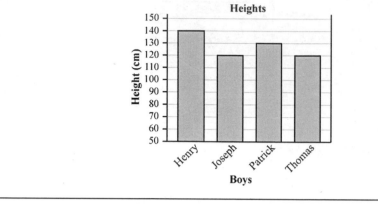

10. Which of the following statements is **true**?

   A. Patrick is 10 cm taller than Henry.

   B. Joseph is 20 cm shorter than Henry.

   C. Thomas is 15 cm shorter than Patrick.

   D. Joseph and Thomas are both 110 cm tall.

Use the following information to answer the next question.

Jake visits Bill's farm and counts the number of different animals he sees. He records the data he collects in a chart.

Animals on Bill's Farm	
Animal	Number
Pigs	20
Ducks	50
Goats	30
Sheep	40

Written Response

11. Create a bar graph that displays the data Jake collected, using many-to-one correspondence.

    Justify the choice of interval you are using.

    Remember to label the title and axes on your graph.

ANSWERS AND SOLUTIONS – UNIT TEST

1. B	4. 57	7. A	10. B
2. D	5. B	8. D	11. WR
3. 8	6. C	9. D	

1. B

If Priya and Kalen each received 20 cards, then each ♥ in the graph represents 4 cards.

Since Priya and Kalen each have 5 hearts to represent 20 cards, you need to divide 20 by 5 to determine the number that each heart represents: 20 ÷ 5 = 4

2. D

If 39 students like running, then each ☺ represents 6 students.

Since running has 6 full faces, divide 39 by 6 to determine the number each face represents: 39 ÷ 6 = 6 R3

This means that each ☺ represents 6 students and each ◖ represents 3 students.

3. 8

If there are 56 books on the 4th shelf, then each 📖 represents 8 books.

Since there are 7 📖📖📖📖📖📖📖 on the 4th shelf, divide 56 by 7 to determine what number each 📖 represents.

56 ÷ 7 = 8

4. 57

A total of 57 students voted for a favourite muffin.

There are 19 pictures of muffins. 19 × 3 = 57

5. B

The salesman sold a total of 45 white and blue cars.

White cars:
Multiply 4 × 5 = 20
or count by 5s for four counts.
5, 10, 15, 20

Blue cars:
Multiply 5 × 5 = 25
or count by 5s for five counts.
5, 10, 15, 20, 25

Add the two sums together. 20 + 25 = 45

6. C

Buildings C and F are taller than 10 metres and shorter than 20 metres.

Building C is about 17 metres tall.
Building F is about 13 metres tall.

Be careful not to be tricked by Building B and Building E.
Building B is exactly 10 m high, not taller than 10 m.
Building E is exactly 20 m high, not shorter than 20 m.

7. A

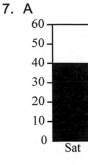

This bar shows the number of seed packages sold on Saturday (40 packages).

First, read the bars in the bargraph determine the number of packages sold each day.

Monday: 45

Tuesday: 40

Wednesday: 30

Thursday: 45

Friday: 50

45 + 40 + 30 + 45 + 50 = 210

There were 210 seed packages sold from Monday to Friday.

Subtract 210 from 250 to find the number of packages sold on Saturday. 250 − 210 = 40

8. D

The statement that is **true** is "there were 10 fewer cupcakes sold than ice-cream cones".

Example strategy
Ice-cream cones: 6 × 10 = 60
Ice pops: 8 × 10 = 80
Cupcakes: 5 × 10 = 50

Choice A is incorrect because
60 + 80 + 50 = 190

Choice B is incorrect because there were 80 icepops and 50 cupcakes.

Choice C is incorrect because
80 − 60 = 20

Choice D is correct because 60 − 50 = 10

9. D

Ted collected twice as many quarters as Jim.

Jim collected 35 quarters.

Multiply 35 by 2 to find the number that is twice as much as 35. 35 × 2 = 70

The bar that represents the number of quarters Ted collected ends at 70.

10. B

The statement that is **true** is "Joseph is 20 cm shorter than Henry."

The top of each bar shows how tall each boy is. If you order the heights from greatest to least and place them in a table, it may be easier to evaluate the statements.

Name	Height in cm
Henry	140
Patrick	130
Joseph	120
Thomas	120

Henry is 140 cm tall and Joseph is 120 cm tall.
140 − 120 = 20

That means that Joseph is 20 cm shorter than Henry or that Henry is 20 cm taller than Joseph.

11. WR

Example graph

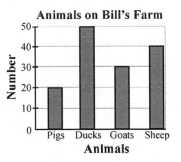

Example justification
I chose to use an interval of 10 because all the numbers (20, 30, 40, 50) are two-digit even numbers that end in 0. As a result, I only needed five intervals to make my graph. The graph is small, but clear and readable.

NOTES

KEY Strategies for Success on Tests

KEY STRATEGIES FOR SUCCESS ON TESTS

THINGS TO CONSIDER WHEN TAKING A TEST

It is normal to feel anxious before you write a test. You can manage this anxiety by using the following strategies:

- Think positive thoughts. Imagine yourself doing well on the test.

- Make a conscious effort to relax by taking several slow, deep, controlled breaths. Concentrate on the air going in and out of your body.

- Before you begin the test, ask questions if you are unsure of anything.

- Jot down key words or phrases from any instructions your teacher gives you.

- Look over the entire test to find out the number and kinds of questions on the test.

- Read each question closely, and reread if necessary.

- Pay close attention to key vocabulary words. Sometimes, these words are **bolded** or *italicized*, and they are usually important words in the question.

- If you are putting your answers on an answer sheet, mark your answers carefully. Always print clearly. If you wish to change an answer, erase the mark completely, and ensure that your final answer is darker than the one you have erased.

- Use highlighting to note directions, key words, and vocabulary that you find confusing or that are important to answering the question.

- Double-check to make sure you have answered everything before handing in your test.

- When taking tests, students often overlook the easy words. Failure to pay close attention to these words can result in an incorrect answer. One way to avoid this is to be aware of these words and to underline, circle, or highlight them while you are taking the test.

- Even though some words are easy to understand, they can change the meaning of the entire question, so it is important that you pay attention to them. Here are some examples.

all	always	most likely	probably	best	not
difference	usually	except	most	unlikely	likely

Example

1. Which of the following expressions is **incorrect**?

   A. $3 + 2 \geq 5$

   B. $4 - 3 < 2$

   C. $5 \times 4 < 15$

   D. $6 \times 3 \geq 18$

TEST PREPARATION AND TEST-TAKING SKILLS

HELPFUL STRATEGIES FOR ANSWERING MULTIPLE-CHOICE QUESTIONS

A multiple-choice question gives you some information and then asks you to select an answer from four choices. Each question has one correct answer. The other choices are distractors, which are incorrect.

The following strategies can help you when answering multiple-choice questions:

- Quickly skim through the entire test. Find out how many questions there are, and plan your time accordingly.

- Read and reread questions carefully. Underline key words, and try to think of an answer before looking at the choices.

- If there is a graphic, look at the graphic, read the question, and go back to the graphic. Then, you may want to underline the important information from the question.

- Carefully read the choices. Read the question first and then each choice that goes with it.

- When choosing an answer, try to eliminate those choices that are clearly wrong or do not make sense.

- Some questions may ask you to select the best answer. These questions will always include words like *best*, *most appropriate,* or *most likely.* All of the choices will be correct to some degree, but one of the choices will be better than the others in some way. Carefully read all four choices before choosing the answer you think is the best.

- If you do not know the answer, or if the question does not make sense to you, it is better to guess than to leave it blank.

- Do not spend too much time on any one question. Make a mark (*) beside a difficult question, and come back to it later. If you are leaving a question to come back to later, make sure you also leave the space on the answer sheet, if you are using one.

- Remember to go back to the difficult questions at the end of the test; sometimes, clues are given throughout the test that will provide you with answers.

- Note any negative words like *no* or *not*, and be sure your answer fits the question.

- Before changing an answer, be sure you have a very good reason to do so.

- Do not look for patterns on your answer sheet, if you are using one.

HELPFUL STRATEGIES FOR ANSWERING WRITTEN-RESPONSE QUESTIONS

A written response requires you to respond to a question or directive indicated by words such as explain, predict, list, describe, show your work, solve, or calculate. The following strategies can help you when answering written-response questions:

- Read and reread the question carefully.

- Recognize and pay close attention to directing words such as *explain*, *show your work*, and *describe*.

- Underline key words and phrases that indicate what is required in your answer, such as *explain*, *estimate*, *answer*, *calculate*, or *show your work*.

- Write down rough, point-form notes regarding the information you want to include in your answer.

- Think about what you want to say, and organize information and ideas in a coherent and concise manner within the time limit you have for the question.

- Be sure to answer every part of the question that is asked.

- Include as much information as you can when you are asked to explain your thinking.

- Include a picture or diagram if it will help to explain your thinking.

- Try to put your final answer to a problem in a complete sentence to be sure it is reasonable.

- Reread your response to ensure you have answered the question.

- Ask yourself if your answer makes sense.

- Ask yourself if your answer sounds right.

- Use appropriate subject vocabulary and terms in your response.

ABOUT MATHEMATICS TESTS

WHAT YOU NEED TO KNOW ABOUT MATHEMATICS TESTS

To do well on a mathematics test, you need to understand and apply your knowledge of mathematical concepts. Reading skills can also make a difference in how well you perform. Reading skills can help you follow instructions and find key words, as well as read graphs, diagrams, and tables. They can also help you solve mathematics problems.

Mathematics tests usually have two types of questions: questions that ask for understanding of mathematics ideas and questions that test how well you can solve mathematics problems.

HOW YOU CAN PREPARE FOR MATHEMATICS TESTS

The following strategies are particular to preparing for and writing mathematics tests:

- Know how to use your calculator, and, if it is allowed, use your own for the test.

- Note taking is a good way to review and study important information from your class notes and textbook.

- Sketch a picture of the problem, procedure, or term. Drawing is helpful for learning and remembering concepts.

- Check your answer to practice questions by working backward to the beginning. You can find the beginning by going step by step in reverse order.

- Use the following steps when answering questions with graphics (pictures, diagrams, tables, or graphs):

  1. Read the title of the graphic and any key words.

  2. Read the test question carefully to figure out what information you need to find in the graphic.

  3. Go back to the graphic to find the information you need.

  4. Decide which operation is needed.

- Always pay close attention when pressing the keys on your calculator. Repeat the procedure a second time to be sure you pressed the correct keys.

TEST PREPARATION COUNTDOWN

If you develop a plan for studying and test preparation, you will perform well on tests.

Here is a general plan to follow seven days before you write a test.

COUNTDOWN: 7 DAYS BEFORE THE TEST

1. Use "Finding Out about the Test" to help you make your own personal test preparation plan.

2. Review the following information:

   – Areas to be included on the test

   – Types of test items

   – General and specific test tips

3. Start preparing for the test at least seven days before the test. Develop your test preparation plan, and set time aside to prepare and study.

COUNTDOWN: 6, 5, 4, 3, 2 DAYS BEFORE THE TEST

1. Review old homework assignments, quizzes, and tests.

2. Rework problems on quizzes and tests to make sure you still know how to solve them.

3. Correct any errors made on quizzes and tests.

4. Review key concepts, processes, formulas, and vocabulary.

5. Create practice test questions for yourself, and answer them. Work out many sample problems.

COUNTDOWN: THE NIGHT BEFORE THE TEST

1. Use the night before the test for final preparation, which includes reviewing and gathering materials needed for the test before going to bed.

2. Most importantly, get a good night's rest, and know you have done everything possible to do well on the test.

TEST DAY

1. Eat a healthy and nutritious breakfast.

2. Ensure you have all the necessary materials.

3. Think positive thoughts, such as "I can do this," "I am ready," and "I know I can do well."

4. Arrive at your school early, so you are not rushing, which can cause you anxiety and stress.

SUMMARY OF HOW TO BE SUCCESSFUL DURING A TEST

You may find some of the following strategies useful for writing a test:

- Take two or three deep breaths to help you relax.

- Read the directions carefully, and underline, circle, or highlight any important words.

- Look over the entire test to understand what you will need to do.

- Budget your time.

- Begin with an easy question or a question you know you can answer correctly rather than follow the numerical question order of the test.

- If you cannot remember how to answer a question, try repeating the deep breathing and physical relaxation activities. Then, move on to visualization and positive self-talk to get yourself going.

- When answering questions with graphics (pictures, diagrams, tables, or graphs), look at the question carefully, and use the following steps:

    1. Read the title of the graphic and any key words.

    2. Read the test question carefully to figure out what information you need to find in the graphic.

    3. Go back to the graphic to find the information you need.

- Write down anything you remember about the subject on the reverse side of your test paper. This activity sometimes helps to remind you that you do know something and are capable of writing the test.

- Look over your test when you have finished, and double-check your answers to be sure you did not forget anything.

NOTES

PRACTICE TEST

1. The expanded notation that represents the numeral 9 709 is
   A. 900 + 70 + 9
   B. 9 000 + 70 + 9
   C. 9 000 + 700 + 9
   D. 9 000 + 700 + 90

2. In the numeral 9 693, the value of the digit 6 is
   A. 60
   B. 69
   C. 600
   D. 693

Use the following information to answer the next question.

Rafe makes the following number line. He asks his friend to tell him what number the letter *Z* represents.

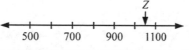

3. Which of the following numbers does the letter *Z* represent?
   A. 1 000
   B. 1 005
   C. 1 050
   D. 1 075

Use the following information to answer the next question.

Julia writes an ordered sequence of numbers with one number missing.
The missing number is represented by the letter *R*.
2 987, 2 997, *R*, 3 017, 3 027

Numerical Response

4. The letter *R* represents the number _____.

Use the following information to answer the next question.

Students at York Elementary School put on a play for the community.

- On Friday, 572 people attended the play.
- On Saturday, 753 people attended the play.
- On Sunday, 601 people attended the play.

5. Using the strategy of compensation, about how many people attended the play over the three days?
   A. 1 700
   B. 1 800
   C. 1 900
   D. 2 000

There are 3 000 coloured counting chips in a bucket. There are 1 654 blue chips, 509 green chips, and 753 yellow chips. The rest of the counting chips are red.

6. How many of the chips are red?

   A. 84

   B. 94

   C. 1 196

   D. 2 916

   Written Response

7. Becca says that $100 \times 0 = 100$.

   Paula says that $100 \times 0 = 1\,000$.

   Lynette says that $100 \times 0 = 0$.

   Who is correct?

   Explain the property of multiplying a number by 0 when determining an answer to a multiplication problem.

8. When Jenna multiplies $8 \times 7 = K$, she uses the strategy of skip counting from a known fact.

   Which of the following skip counting patterns from a known fact will help Jenna get the correct answer?

   A. 12, 20, 28…

   B. 14, 21, 27…

   C. 16, 23, 30…

   D. 24, 32, 40…

9. Using the distributive property of multiplication, the problem 9 × 175 can be shown as

A. (9 × 1) + (9 × 7) + (9 × 5)   B. (9 × 10) + (9 × 70) + (9 × 50)

C. (9 × 100) + (9 × 17) + (9 × 5)   D. (9 × 100) + (9 × 70) + (9 × 5)

10. Mira bought 6 packages of lined paper for school. Each package had 175 sheets of paper.

The **best** estimate of the number of sheets of paper Mira bought is

A. 600   B. 1 200

C. 1 400   D. 1 500

Use the following information to answer the next question.

In a division problem, the dividend is 92. The quotient is 11 with a remainder of 4.

11. What is the divisor?

A. 6   B. 7

C. 8   D. 9

12. Which of the following sets of fractions is ordered from least to greatest?

A. $\dfrac{2}{8}, \dfrac{4}{8}, \dfrac{7}{8}, \dfrac{8}{8}$ B. $\dfrac{1}{8}, \dfrac{3}{8}, \dfrac{6}{8}, \dfrac{4}{8}$

C. $\dfrac{5}{8}, \dfrac{4}{8}, \dfrac{3}{8}, \dfrac{2}{8}$ D. $\dfrac{8}{8}, \dfrac{2}{8}, \dfrac{4}{8}, \dfrac{6}{8}$

Use the following information to answer the next question.

The given fraction circle has shaded parts and parts that are not shaded.

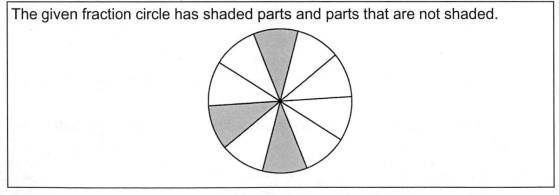

13. The fraction that represents the parts that are **not** shaded is

A. $\dfrac{7}{3}$ B. $\dfrac{3}{7}$ C. $\dfrac{3}{10}$ D. $\dfrac{7}{10}$

Numerical Response

14. Write a fraction that is greater than $\frac{1}{4}$, less than $\frac{1}{2}$, and has the number 1 as a numerator._____

15. The decimal 0.4 is represented by the shaded parts of which of the following circles?

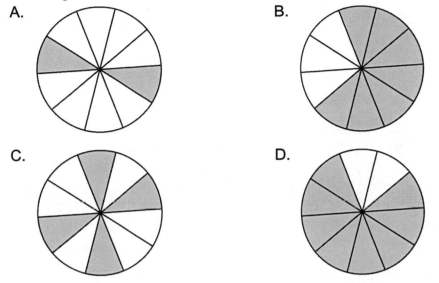

A.

B.

C.

D.

Use the following information to answer the next question.

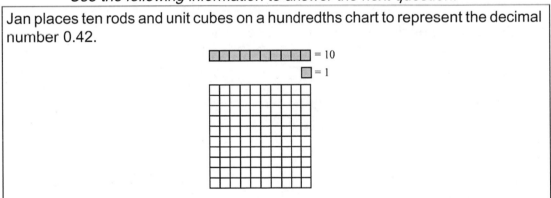

Jan places ten rods and unit cubes on a hundredths chart to represent the decimal number 0.42.

$\blacksquare\blacksquare\blacksquare\blacksquare\blacksquare\blacksquare\blacksquare\blacksquare\blacksquare\blacksquare$ = 10
$\blacksquare$ = 1

16. Which of the following combinations of ten rods and unit cubes will represent the decimal number 0.42?

    A. 3 ten rods and 2 unit cubes   B. 3 ten rods and 12 unit cubes

    C. 4 ten rods and 3 unit cubes   D. 4 ten rods and 12 unit cubes

Written Response

17. Explain the meaning of each digit in the number 1 111.11.

    You may use a place value chart to help you explain.

18. Which of the following sets of decimals and fractions are equivalent?

    A. 0.05 and $\frac{50}{100}$

    B. 0.04 and $\frac{4}{10}$

    C. 0.60 and $\frac{60}{100}$

    D. 0.30 and $\frac{3}{100}$

Use the following information to answer the next question.

Ron had $15.00 when he went to the carnival. When he came home, he had $3.21 left.

19. How much money did Ron spend at the carnival?

    A. $12.79

    B. $12.21

    C. $11.79

    D. $11.69

Use the following information to answer the next question.

Using the given number chart, Jia started with the number 12 and circled numbers to follow a particular pattern rule. She forgot to circle one number to complete the pattern.

1	2	3	4	5	6	7	8	9	10
11	(12)	13	14	15	16	17	18	19	20
21	22	23	(24)	25	26	27	28	29	30
31	32	33	34	35	(36)	37	38	39	40
41	42	43	44	45	46	47	(48)	49	50
51	52	53	54	55	56	57	58	59	(60)
61	62	63	64	65	66	67	68	69	70
71	72	73	74	75	76	77	78	79	80
81	82	83	(84)	85	86	87	88	89	90
91	92	93	94	95	(96)	97	98	99	100

20. The number Jia forgot to circle to complete the pattern is

A. 62   B. 72

C. 73   D. 76

Use the following information to answer the next question.

The numbers in this table create a pattern.

1st	2nd	3rd	4th	5th	6th	7th
130	120	111	103	?	?	?

Numerical Response

21. If the pattern continues, the 7th number will be _____.

Use the following information to answer the next question.

Miss Bandar gave Rob the pattern of numbers in the given chart. She asked him to complete the pattern and then represent the completed pattern using numbered tiles.

3	6	9	12	?	?	?	?

Rob arranged the numbered tiles in a square to show the completed pattern of numbers from the chart.

He started at the top left corner of the square. He placed a blank tile after each numbered tile.

22. Which of the following squares represents the completed pattern of numbers from the chart?

A.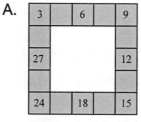

B.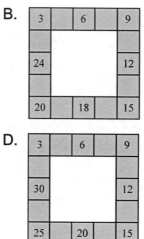

C.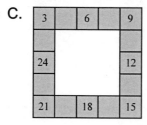

D.

Use the following information to answer the next question.

Deepa is a baker. She uses this chart to help her plan how many cups of flour and how many eggs she needs when she bakes several same-size cakes.

Number of Cakes	Cups of Flour	Number of Eggs
1	3	2
2	6	4
3	9	6
4	12	8

23. To bake 10 cakes Deepa will need

    A. 24 cups of flour and 16 eggs   **B.** 27 cups of flour and 20 eggs

    C. 30 cups of flour and 16 eggs   **D.** 30 cups of flour and 20 eggs

Use the following information to answer the next question.

Jenny, Chris, and Mario each have a different favourite juice:
orange, cherry, apple.

- Jenny and Mario do not like orange juice.
- Jenny only likes red juice.

24. Which of the following charts shows the favourite juice of each child?

A.

	Orange	Cherry	Apple
Jenny	X	✓	X
Chris	X	X	✓
Mario	X	✓	X

B.

	Orange	Cherry	Apple
Jenny	X	X	✓
Chris	✓	X	X
Mario	X	✓	X

C.

	Orange	Cherry	Apple
Jenny	X	X	✓
Chris	✓	X	X
Mario	X	X	✓

D.

	Orange	Cherry	Apple
Jenny	X	✓	X
Chris	✓	X	X
Mario	X	X	✓

25. Mrs. Morris is organizing a dinner for her family's reunion. There will be 50 people attending the dinner, and Mrs. Morris plans to seat 5 people to a table.

The equation that can be used to find how many tables Mrs. Morris needs is

A. $50 - n = 5$

B. $5 + n = 50$

C. $5 \times 50 = n$

D. $50 \div 5 = n$

Use the following information to answer the next question.

Carrie has a total of 30 buttons. She places them in 6 groups, making an array.

⊕⊕⊕⊕⊕
⊕⊕⊕⊕⊕
⊕⊕⊕⊕⊕
⊕⊕⊕⊕⊕
⊕⊕⊕⊕⊕
⊕⊕⊕⊕⊕

Written Response

26. How many buttons does she place in each group?

Let the letter *R* represent the unknown, which is the number of buttons in each group.

Write four different equations that can represent the array of buttons.

27. In the equation $144 = 6 \times K$ what number does *K* represent?
    A. 20   B. 22
    C. 24   D. 26

Use the following information to answer the next question.

On Saturday Marco's piano lessons end at the time shown on the clock.

28. Marco's piano lessons end at
    A. 10:53 A.M.   B. 10:54 A.M.
    C. 11:07 A.M.   D. 11:53 A.M.

Use the following information to answer the next question.

On Saturday, Paul has a soccer practise that starts at 17:15.

29. Another way of showing the time the soccer practise starts is
    A. 5:15 A.M.   B. 5:15 P.M.
    C. 7:15 A.M.   D. 7:15 P.M.

| Written Response |

30. Using the format **dd/mm/yy**, write the date shown on the calendar page.

June 2007						
S	M	T	W	T	F	S
	1	2	3	4	5	6
7	8	9	10	11	12	13
14	15	16	17	18	19	20
21	22	23	24	25	26	27
28	29	30				

Use the following information to answer the next question.

Mr. Li estimates the area of a rug he wants to buy.
He uses a piece of cardboard that is 1 m² to help him estimate the area.

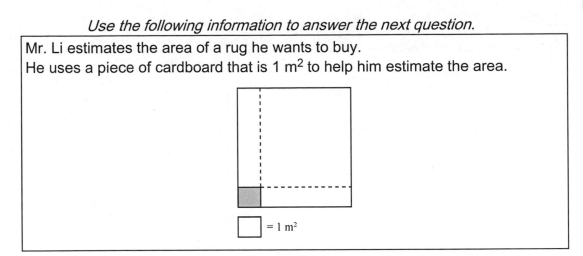

☐ = 1 m²

31. The **best** estimate of the area of the rug is

A. 18 m²
B. 22 m²
C. 24 m²
D. 30 m²

32. Which of the following nets will fold into a right triangular prism?

A.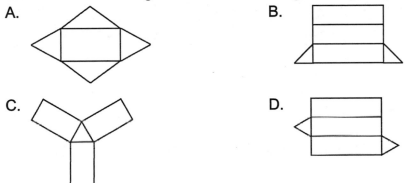

B.

C.

D.

Use the following information to answer the next question.

Rick says that the given net will fold into a right triangular prism.
Kate says that the given net will fold into a right rectangular prism.

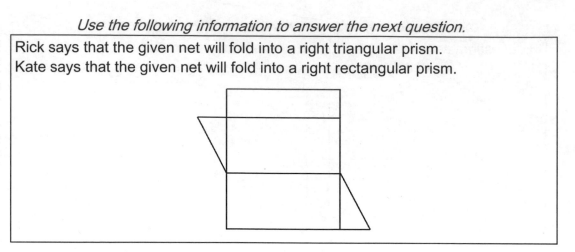

Written Response

33. Who is correct? Explain your answer using mathematical language.

Use the following information to answer the next question.

In art class, Josh drew borders around six of his animal pictures.

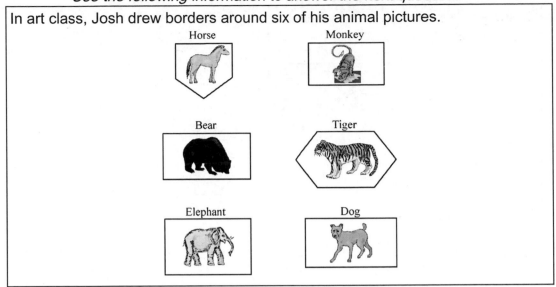

34. Which two animal pictures have borders that are congruent?

    A. Bear and dog   B. Horse and tiger

    C. Bear and elephant   D. Monkey and elephant

Use the following information to answer the next question.

Clayton plans to draw a line of symmetry through as many of the given numbers as possible.

$$1 \ 2 \ 3 \ 4 \ 5$$

$$6 \ 7 \ 8 \ 9 \ 0$$

35. Through how many numbers can Clayton draw a line of symmetry?

    A. 3 numbers   B. 4 numbers

    C. 5 numbers   D. 6 numbers

Use the following information to answer the next question.

On a piece of grid paper, Ruth drew half of a 2-D shape.

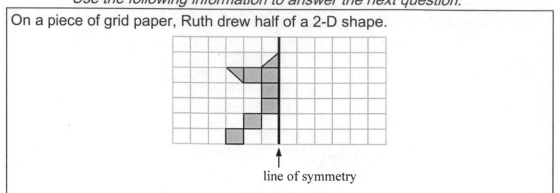

line of symmetry

Written Response

36. Complete Ruth's picture by drawing the other half of the shape on the right side of the line of symmetry.

Use the following information to answer the next question.

A group of five students read a total of 75 books. The graph below shows the number of books that each student read.

Books Read

Number of books

Rena   Ted   Aldo   Cody   Dara

Student

37. Each line on the graph represents
   A. 2 books
   B. 3 books
   C. 4 books
   D. 5 books

Use the following information to answer the next question.

The given graph shows the number of people who chose one of four genres of books as their favourite genre to read.

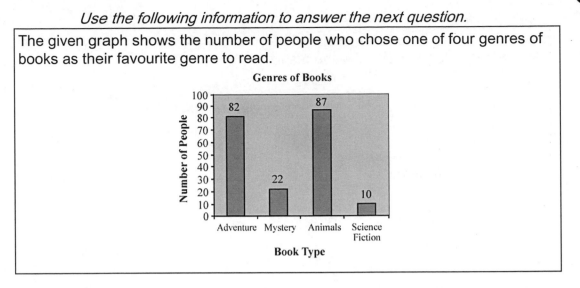

Genres of Books

| Written Response |

38. Describe the correspondence used in the graph.

Explain why many-to-one correspondence was a better choice to use than one-to-one correspondence.

Use the following information to answer the next question.

Clint surveys his classmates to see what types of activities they enjoy the most. He made a pictograph to show the results.

Activity	Number of Students
Reading	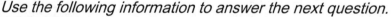
Watching TV	
Playing Sports	
Making Crafts	
Playing games	

Key: ![figure] = 4 students

39. Which of the following conclusions **cannot** be made by using the information in the pictograph?

  A. A half figure represents 2 students.

  B. Fewer students enjoy making crafts than playing sports.

  C. There were 46 students who participated in the survey.

  D. There are 3 students who have more than one favourite activity.

Use the following information to answer the next question.

This graph shows the amount of snow that fell from October to March.

40. Which of the following months had the **least** combined amount of snowfall?

  A. October and February

  B. November and January

  C. December and February

  D. December and March

Use the following information to answer the next question.

Every day for one week, between 5:00 P.M. and 6:00 P.M., Avi counted the number of cars that passed through an intersection near his house. He made this bar graph to show the results.

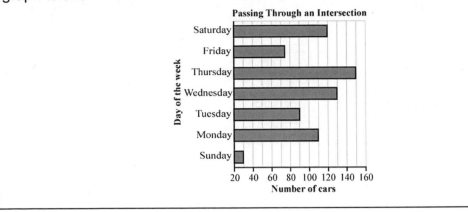

Numerical Response

41. The number of cars that passed through the intersection on Friday was _____.

ANSWERS AND SOLUTIONS – PRACTICE TEST

1. C	10. B	19. C	28. A	37. B
2. C	11. C	20. B	29. B	38. WR
3. C	12. A	21. 85	30. WR	39. D
4. 3007	13. D	22. C	31. D	40. C
5. C	14. 1/3	23. D	32. B	41. 75
6. A	15. C	24. D	33. WR	
7. WR	16. B	25. D	34. A	
8. D	17. WR	26. WR	35. B	
9. D	18. C	27. C	36. WR	

1. C

The expanded notation 9 000 + 700 + 9 represents the numeral 9 709.

In the numeral 9 709, there are 9 thousands, 7 hundreds, 0 tens, and 9 ones.

2. C

In the numeral 9 693, the value of the digit 6 is 600.

In 9 693, there are 9 thousands, 6 hundreds, 9 tens, and 3 ones.

3. C

The letter Z represents the number 1 050.

The numbers on the number line count by 200s.

That means that the ticks between the numbers represent the missing hundreds: 600, 800, 1 000.

The letter Z is halfway between the tick that represents 1 000 and the number 1 100. Half of 100 is 50.

4. 3007

The numbers are ordered in ascending order (lowest to greatest).

The numbers in the sequence grow larger by adding 10 each time. To find the number that R represents, add 10 to 2 997. 2 997 + 10 = 3 007

5. C

About 1 900 people attended the play over the three days.

Compensation Strategy
Use front-end estimation for the first two numbers, but use front-end estimation +1 for the last number.
572 → 500
753 → 700
601 → 700(6 + 1)

Add the three estimates.
500 + 700 + 700 = 1 900

6. A

There are 84 red chips in the bucket.

First, add the number of blue, green, and yellow chips.
1 654 + 509 + 753 = 2 916

Next, subtract the number of blue, green, and yellow chips from the total number to find the number of red chips.
3 000 – 2 916 = 84

7. WR

Lynette is correct. $100 \times 0 = 0$

Example explanation
The property of 0 for multiplication tells you that any number multiplied by 0 will always equal 0. It does not matter how large or small the number is, the product will still be 0.

8. D

The skip counting pattern Jenna can use is 24, 32, 40,…

The known fact that starts the pattern is $8 \times 3 = 24$.

Jenna can then skip count by 8s for 4 more counts [from multiplying by 3 (third count) to multiplying by 7 (seventh count)].

Third count: $24(8 \times 3 = 24)$, 32, 40, 48
Seventh count: $56(8 \times 7 = 56)$

9. D

Using the distributive property, the given problem can be shown as
$(9 \times 100) + (9 \times 70) + (9 \times 5)$.

To apply the distributive property, use place value to break down the number 175 into hundreds, tens, and ones.
$175 = 100 + 70 + 5$

Multiply the hundreds, tens, and ones by 9, then add the three products.

10. B

The best estimate is that Mira bought about 1 200 sheets of paper.

Example estimation
Most estimates end in 0. Since the number 175 is much closer to 200 than to 100, you can estimate that there are about 200 sheets in one package. $175 \rightarrow 200$

To estimate the number of sheets in 6 packages, multiply the estimated number in one package by 6.
$200 \times 6 = 1\ 200$

11. C

The divisor is 8.

Example strategy
One way to solve this problem is to use multiplication to help you estimate the divisor.

If you know that $11 \times 9 = 99$, then you know that the divisor is less than 9, because 92 is less than 99.

If you know that $11 \times 8 = 88$, then you know that the divisor is most likely 8, because 88 is close to but less than 92.

When you subtract 88 from 92, you have 4 left over.
$92 - 88 = 4$
$92 \div 8 = 11\ R4$

12. A

The set of fractions $\frac{2}{8}, \frac{4}{8}, \frac{7}{8}, \frac{8}{8}$ is ordered from least to greatest.

When the denominators are the same number, compare the numerators.

The rule is "the smaller the number, the smaller the fraction."

From smallest number (least) to greatest number, the numerators are 2, 4, 7, 8.

13. D

The fraction that represents the parts that are not shaded is $\frac{7}{10}$.

There are 10 parts altogether, so 10 is the denominator.

There are 7 parts that are not shaded, so 7 is the numerator.

14. 1/3

The fraction $\frac{1}{3}$ is greater than $\frac{1}{4}$, less than $\frac{1}{2}$, and has a numerator of 1.

When the numerators are the same number and the denominators are different numbers, the rule, when comparing fractions, is *the greater the fraction, the smaller the denominator.*

That means that the denominator for the new fraction must be less than 4 and greater than 2, which is the number 3.

In order from least to greatest, the fractions are $\frac{1}{4}, \frac{1}{3}, \frac{1}{2}$.

15. C

The decimal 0.4 is represented by the shaded parts of this circle.

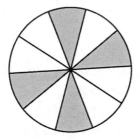

To represent the decimal 0.4, the circle must have 10 equal parts, with 4 of the parts shaded.

16. B

The combination of 3 ten rods and 12 unit cubes will represent the decimal number 0.42.

17. WR

Example explanation

T	H	T	O	•	Tenths	Hundredths
1	1	1	1		1	1
1 000	100	10	1		$\frac{1}{10}$	$\frac{1}{100}$

<u>1</u>111.11: Starting at the left, the first 1 represents 1 000.

1 <u>1</u>11.11: The second 1 represents 100.

1 1<u>1</u>1.11: The third 1 represents 10.

1 11<u>1</u>.11: The fourth 1 represents 1.

1 111.<u>1</u>1: The first 1 to the right of the decimal represents $\frac{1}{10}$.

1 111.1<u>1</u>: The second 1 to the right of the decimal represents $\frac{1}{100}$.

18. C

The decimal 0.60 and the fraction $\frac{60}{100}$ are equivalent.

They can both represent 60 squares on a hundredths grid.

19. C

Ron spent $11.79 at the carnival.

Subtract the amount of money left from the total amount of money to determine the amount spent. When you subtract decimals, remember to line up the decimal points.

You also need to regroup when you subtract these numbers.
$15.00 – $3.21 = $11.79

20. B

The number that Jia forgot to circle is 72.

The pattern rule Jia used is add 12 to each number to get the next number. 60 + 12 = 72

21. 85

The pattern rule used is to subtract 10, then 9, and then 8, to get the numbers 120, 111, and 103.
(130 − 10 = 120)(120 − 9 = 111)
(111 − 8 = 103)

You need to continue the pattern rule and subtract 7, then 6, then 5 to get the next three numbers.
(103 − 7 = 96)(96 − 6 = 90)(90 − 5 = 85)

1st	2nd	3rd
130	120(−10)	111(−9)

4th	5th	6th	7th
103(−8)	96(−7)	90(−6)	85(−5)

22. C

This square represents the completed pattern of numbers from the chart:

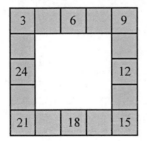

The pattern rule for the numbers in the chart is "add 3 each time."

3	6	9	12	15	18	21	24

23. D

To bake 10 cakes Deepa will need 30 cups of flour and 20 eggs.

The pattern rule for the number of cups of flour is add 3 each time.
3, 6, 9, 12, 15, 18, 21, 24, 27, 30

Another strategy is to multiply the number of cakes by 3. 10 × 3 = 30

The pattern rule for the number of eggs is add 2 each time.
2, 4, 6, 8, 10, 12, 14, 16, 18, 20

Another strategy is to multiply the number of cakes by 2. 10 × 2 = 20

24. D

The following diagram shows the favourite juice of each child.

	Orange	Cherry	Apple
Jenny	X	✓	X
Chris	✓	X	X
Mario	X	X	✓

Since Jenny and Mario do not like orange juice, Chris's favourite drink must be orange.
Since Jenny only likes red juice, her favourite drink must be cherry.
That means that Mario's favourite drink must be apple.

25. D

The equation that can be used to find how many tables Mrs. Morris needs is
50 ÷ 5 = *n*.
50 ÷ 5 = 10

Mrs. Morris needs 10 tables.

26. WR

Example equations
$30 ÷ 6 = R$ or $R = 30 ÷ 6$
$30 ÷ R = 6$ or $6 = 30 ÷ R$
$6 × R = 30$ or $30 = 6 × R$
$R × 6 = 30$ or $30 = R × 6$

27. C

K represents the number 24.

To solve this multiplication problem, use the inverse operation of division.
$144 = 6 × K$
$144 ÷ 6 = K$
$144 ÷ 6 = 24$
$K = 24$
$144 = 6 × 24$

Practice TEST

28. A

Marco's piano lessons end at 10:53.

The hour hand points between 10 and 11. The hour is 10:00. The number 10 is written to the left of the two dots. 6:_____

The minute hand points to 3 ticks after the 10.

Start at the 12 position. Count by fives from the number 1 position to the number 10 position.

5, 10, 15, 20, 25, 30, 35, 40, 45, 50

Then count by ones for the 3 ticks after the 10. ...51, 52, 53.

It is 53 minutes after 10 o'clock or 10:53 A.M.

29. B

Another way of showing the time 17:15 is 5:15 P.M.

To change 24-hour time to 12-hour time, subtract 12 hours from the 17 hours.
17 – 12 = 5

The minutes will stay the same.
In 12-hour time, you need to write P.M. after the noon to midnight hours.

30. WR

Starting with the day, then the month, and then the year (dd/mm/yy), the date on the calendar page is written as 08/06/07.

31. D

The best estimate of the area of the rug is 30 m^2.

Using the size of the given square, you can estimate that 6 rows of same-size squares and 5 columns of same-size squares would cover the surface of the rug.
6 × 5 = 30

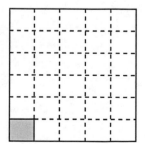

32. B

This net can fold into a right triangular prism.

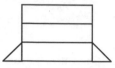

In a right triangular prism, the two triangle bases must have right angles and be congruent.

33. WR

Rick is correct.

Example explanation
The net shown has 3 rectangular faces with 2 triangular bases, one on each side of the row of rectangles. This is how I know that the net will fold into a triangular prism, not a rectangular prism.

Since the triangular bases have right angles, I know that the prism will be a right triangular prism.

34. A

The borders around the bear and dog pictures are congruent (same size and shape).

35. B

Clayton can draw a line of symmetry through 4 of the given numbers.

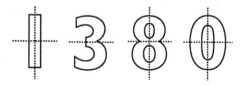

36. **WR**

This diagram shows the mirror image of the half that Ruth drew. It is shaded in a darker colour to help you see the two parts.

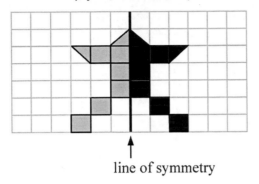

line of symmetry

37. **B**

Each line on the graph represents 3 books. Count the number of spaces of each bar.
Rena—4; Ted—3; Aldo—7; Cody—7; Dara —4
4 + 3 + 7 + 7 + 4 = 25
Since there are three groups of 25 in 75 (25, 50, 75), the lines on the graph count up by 3s.
0, 3, 6, 9, 12, 15, 18, 21, 24

38. **WR**

Many-to-one correspondence with an interval of 10 is used in the given graph.
Example explanation
Using many-to-one correspondence in which each tick represents 10 students makes the graph small so that space is not wasted, but uses numbers that are still easy to see and read.
If one-to-one correspondence had been used, the graph would be very tall because you would need at least 87 ticks. As well, the numbers and ticks would be so crowded that it would be hard to read.

39. **D**

Using the information in the pictograph, you cannot make the conclusion that there are 3 students who have more than one favourite activity.
There is nothing in the information presented that indicates that some students (3) made more than one choice.

40. **C**

Of the choices given, December and February had the least combined amount of snowfall.

Look at where the bars end to determine the amount of snow that fell each month.

Placing the data in a table makes it easier to compare the different combinations.

October and February	30 cm + 5 cm = 35 cm
November and January	15 cm + 25 cm = 40 cm
December and February	20 cm + 5 cm = 25 cm
December and March	20 cm + 10 cm = 30 cm

Of the four numbers (40, 35, 30, 25), 25 is the least number.

41. **75**

On Friday, 75 cars passed through the intersection.

The x-axis starts at 20. Every second line then counts by 20s.
20, 40, 60…160

That means that every line counts by 10s.
20, 30, 40…160

The space halfway between two lines represents a number that ends in 5.
5, 15, 25, 35…155

The bar for Friday ends halfway between the line that represents the number 70 and the numbered line 80.
70, 75, 80

NOTES

GLOSSARY

add To find the sum of two or more numbers. For example, $35 + 12 = 47$.

algorithm An organized set of steps to follow when carrying out a calculation.

analog clock A clock that shows time by hands moving around a centre point.

> A 12-hour clock records hours from 1 to 12, using A.M. for hours from midnight to noon and P.M. for hours from noon to midnight. For example, the time shown on this clock could be 9:20 A.M. or 9:20 P.M.

> A 24-hour clock records the P.M. hours as a continuation of the numbers after 12, from 13 to 24, instead of repeating the numbers 1 to 12. For example, the time shown on this clock is 09:20 (morning time) or 21:20 (afternoon time).

area The number of congruent shapes that cover the surface of a 3-D object or 2-D figure; area is often measured in square units. For example, the area of this shape is 60 sq. units.

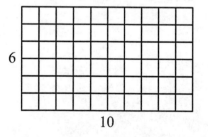

array A grid that shows objects in rows and columns. Arrays can be used to show multiplication or division. For example, this array can represent the following facts:
$3 \times 5 = 15, 5 \times 3 = 15, 15 \div 3 = 5, 15 \div 5 = 3$

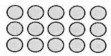

ascending order To order from least to greatest. For example, the following numbers are listed in ascending order: 1 000, 2 000, 3 000.

bar graph A graph that shows data using bars on a grid. Bars can be vertical (see graph in *interval*) or horizontal, as shown below.

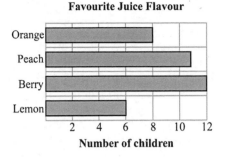

Favourite Juice Flavour

Number of children

base ten blocks (materials) Units, ten rods, hundred flats, and thousand cubes that can be used to represent numbers.

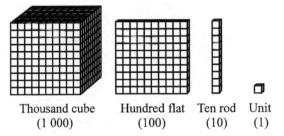

| Thousand cube | Hundred flat | Ten rod | Unit |
| (1 000) | (100) | (10) | (1) |

benchmark A standard of measure set so other measures can be compared to it.

For example, when you compare the fraction $\dfrac{3}{10}$ to the benchmarks of 0 and 1, the fraction $\dfrac{3}{10}$ is closer to 0 than to 1.

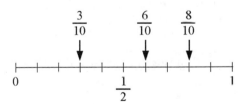

Carroll diagram A table used to organize information that involves two or more choices. Checks ($\sqrt{}$) and "x"s are usually used to represent responses of "yes" or "no."

	Orange	Apple	Banana
Tim	x	$\sqrt{}$	x
Lynn	x	x	$\sqrt{}$
Ken	$\sqrt{}$	x	x

chart An organized way to display data.

Colour	Tally Results	Total
Blue	||||	4
Red	‖‖‖	5
Yellow	‖‖‖ |	6

compensation A strategy for adjusting an estimated sum or difference of two or more numbers to make the estimated answer closer to the actual answer. For example, one strategy for compensation could be to use the first digit for the first two numbers and adjust the third number by using the first digit plus 1. <u>3</u>31 + <u>2</u>10 + <u>6</u>47 = <u>3</u>00 + <u>2</u>00 + <u>7</u>00

congruent Figures that have the same size and shape. The three triangles shown are all congruent to each other even though they have been rotated. When a figure has a line of symmetry, two congruent shapes can be found on either side of the line of symmetry.

data Facts or pieces of information collected about people or things. Data can be collected through a survey.

data values The numbers in a chart or table; the numbers the bars or pictures represent on a graph. For example, the data values shown in this graph are 24 (cars), 15 (vans), and 12 (trucks).

1 picture = 3 vehicles

decimal number A number with one or more digits to the right of a decimal point. A decimal number shows parts of a whole in tenths or hundredths. For example, the place value chart shows the decimal number 1.04.

Ones	Decimal	Tenths	Hundredths
1	●	0	4

denominator The bottom number of a fraction. The total number of parts.

$$\frac{3}{4}$$ — numerator
— denominator

descending order To order from greatest to least. For example, the following numbers are listed in descending order: 5 500, 5 000, 4 500, 4 000.

diagonal On a slant. For example, a diagonal line on a square could be from one corner to the opposite corner. See diagram for *line of symmetry*.

digit Any of the numbers 0, 1, 2, 3, 4, 5, 6, 7, 8, 9. Some numbers have only one digit, while others are made up of many digits. For example, the number 8 293 has four digits.

digital clock A clock that shows time in numbers. The numbers to the left of the two dots (:) show the hour. The numbers to the right of the two dots (:) show the number of minutes after the hour. The time shown on this clock would be read as "thirty minutes after eight o'clock" or "eight thirty."

distributive property To multiply each place value of a larger number by the multiplier and then to add the products. For example, $2 \times 48 = (2 \times 40) + (2 \times 8)$.

divide To find how many equal groups can be made out of a total number of items or how many items will be in each equal group. For example, a total number of 63 cookies can be divided into 9 equal groups with 7 cookies in each group $\rightarrow 63 \div 9 = 7$.

dividend The number that is being divided in a division problem. For example, in the equation, $8 \div 4 = 2$, the dividend is the number 8.

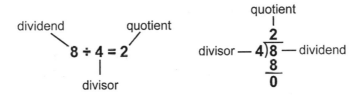

divisor The number of groups or number in each group in a division problem. For example, in the equation $8 \div 4 = 2$, the number 8 represents the total number and the number 4 represents the divisor. See diagram for *dividend*.

doubling A mental strategy for multiplying or dividing; it means to add the same number to itself or to multiply a number by 2. For example, $9 + 9$ or $9 \times 2 = 18$.

doubling plus a group A mental strategy for multiplying or dividing; it means to multiply a number by 2 (double), and then add one more of the same number. For example, $7 \times 2 = 14$ (double), $14 + 7 = 21$ (doubling plus a group).

edge The place where two faces join together on a three-dimensional solid or object.

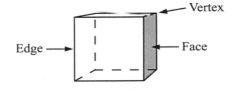

equation A number sentence that uses an equal sign (=) to show that two amounts are equal. For example, $3 \times 4 = 12$. Sometimes a letter or symbol is used to show an unknown number in an equation. For example, $7 \times \square = 21$
$$7 \times 3 = 21$$

equivalent Having the same value. For example, 0.4 is equivalent to $\dfrac{4}{10}$.

estimation An approximate answer; not an exact answer. For example, an estimate of the sum of 4 310 + 3 014 can be 7 000.

expanded notation A way to describe or represent numbers; the sum of the place values in a number. For example, the expanded notation form of the number 7 521 is 7 000 + 500 + 20 + 1.

extend a pattern To continue a pattern. For example, to extend or continue this number pattern, 1, 2, 4, 8, __, __, multiply 8 by 2 (8 × 2 = 16) and 16 by 2. (16 × 2 = 32).

face A flat surface on a three-dimensional (3-D) solid. A face is described by using the name of its two-dimensional (2-D) shape. For example, a cube has 6 square faces. See diagram for *edge*.

fact family A set of related multiplication and division facts or related subtraction and addition facts. For example, these four facts make up a fact family. They use the same three numbers.

6 × 9 = 54	54 ÷ 9 = 6
9 × 6 = 54	54 ÷ 6 = 9

fraction A part of a set or a part of a whole. All parts must be equal in size. For example, the fraction that represents 1 shaded part out of a total of 3 equal parts is $\frac{1}{3}$ (one-third).

front end estimation A strategy for estimating, using the first one or two digits (greatest value) of a number. For example, when using front end estimation, the number <u>4</u> 809 becomes <u>4</u> 000.

geometric pattern A pattern made out of shapes and figures.

greatest value The highest number in a group of numbers. For example, in the numbers 3 275, 6 200, and 5 280, the number with the greatest value is 6 200.

halving A mental strategy for multiplying or dividing; to divide by 2. For example, if you know that 24 ÷ 4 = 6, then you know that 12 ÷ 4 = 3.

halving and subtracting one group A mental strategy for multiplying or dividing; to divide by 2 and then subtract one more group. For example, if you know that 6 × 8 = 48, then 3 × 8 = 24, and 2 × 8 = 16 (subtracting one more group: 24 – 8 = 16).

horizontal To the left or right; across. For example, _____.

interval The distance between two numbers on the scale of a graph. On this graph, the interval is 10; each square represents 10 insects.

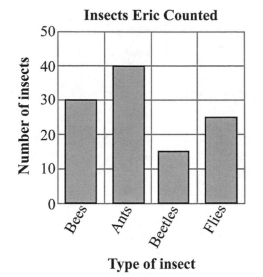

Insects Eric Counted

inverse operation An opposite operation; division is inverse to multiplication and subtraction is inverse to addition. For example, since $5 \times 6 = 30$, then $30 \div 6 = 5$. An inverse operation can be used to check an answer. For example, to check if $72 \div 8 = 9$, multiply 9×8 to see if you get 72.

key The part of the graph that explains the value of the symbol used. In this graph, the key explains that each face represents 2 children.

Favourite Summer Activities				
Soccer	☺	☺	☺	
Baseball	☺	☺	☺	☺
Swimming	☺	☺	☺	
Biking	☺	☺		
Hiking	☺	☺		

Key: ☺ represents 2 children

least value The smallest number in a group of numbers. For example, in the numbers 9 979, 6 909, and 8 500, the number with the least value is 6 909.

line of symmetry A horizontal, vertical, or diagonal line that divides a figure into two congruent parts. A figure may have more than one line of symmetry or may have no line of symmetry. For example, a square has four lines of symmetry.

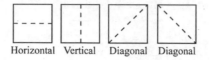

Horizontal   Vertical   Diagonal   Diagonal

many-to-one correspondence When one square on a bar graph or one picture on a pictograph represents more than one number or item.

mental strategy A plan used to help solve a problem in your head. For example, when adding $1 + 3 + 9 + 7$, group numbers that equal 10 together $\rightarrow 1 + 9 = 10, 3 + 7 = 10$. It is easier to add $10 + 10$ in your head than $1 + 3 + 9 + 7$.

multiply To find the total number of items when the number of equal groups and the number of items in each group is known. For example, if there are 3 bags with 4 candies in each bag, multiply to find the total number of candies $\rightarrow 3 \times 4 = 12$.

multiplier The number you are multiplying by. For example, in the multiplication problem, $3 \times 4 = 12$, the multiplier is 4.

net A 2-D shape that can be folded into a 3-D object. A 3-D object can have more than one net. For example, both nets shown can fold into the same rectangular prism.

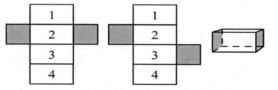

number line A line with evenly spaced numbers shown on the line. For example, this number shows skip counting by fives.

one count

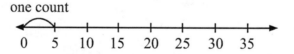

number pattern A pattern made out of numbers. For example, 2, 12, 22, 32.

numeral A number made up of digits (symbols). For example, the digits 1, 6, 8, and 3 can be put together to make the numeral 1 683.

numerator The top number of a fraction; the number of parts that are being considered. See diagram in *denominator*.

pattern An ordered set of numbers, figures, or actions that follows a rule. For example, the following numbers form a pattern: 7, 8, 8, 7, 8, 8, 7, 8, 8,

pattern that increases A pattern that grows in number. For example, this number pattern adds 5 each time to make it grow: 5, 10, 15, 20.

pattern that decreases A pattern that shrinks (gets smaller) in number.
For example, this number pattern subtracts 3 each time to make it shrink: 27, 24, 21.

pattern that repeats A pattern made by using the same set of numbers or figures over and over.
For example, in the pattern shown the same three figures are repeated.

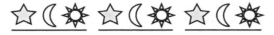

pattern rule The part of a pattern that repeats (sometimes called a unit or a core); a statement that explains a pattern or tells how to make a pattern. For example, in the pattern 1, 5, 9, 13, the pattern rule is *Start at 1. Add 4 each time*.

perimeter The distance all around a figure. To find perimeter, add the lengths of all the sides. For example, the distance all around this figure is 4 m + 2 m + 4 m + 2 m = 12 m.

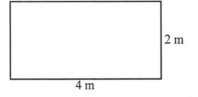

pictograph A graph that uses pictures or symbols to display data. See graph in *key*.

place value chart A chart that shows the position of a digit in a number. For example, in the number 3 546.2, the digit 3 is in the thousands place, 5 is in the hundreds place, 4 is in the tens place, 6 is in the ones place, 2 is in the tenths place.

	TH	H	T	O	•	Tenths
Position →	3	5	4	6	•	2
Value →	3 000	500	40	6		$\frac{2}{10}$

prism A solid with two opposite and congruent bases; the shape of the bases gives the prism its name.

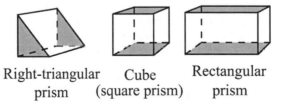

Right-triangular   Cube   Rectangular
prism   (square prism)   prism

product The answer to a multiplication problem. For example, in the problem 7 × 8 = 56, the number 56 is the product.

property of 0 for multiplication Any number multiplied by zero will equal zero.
For example, 12 × 0 = 0

property of 1 for multiplication Any number multiplied by 1 will equal that number.
For example, 9 × 1 = 9

property of 1 for division Any number divided by 1 will equal that number. For example, $15 \div 1 = 15$

quotient The answer to a division problem. See diagram in *dividend*.

referent Using an object that has about the same size and shape as a particular measurement to determine the area of a shape. For example, a die can be used as a referent when measuring area in square centimetres, because a die is about 1 cm long on all sides.

regroup To exchange amounts of an equal value to rename a number. For example, 4 ten rods and 12 units can be regrouped to 5 ten rods and 2 units. Both have a value of 52.

relationship The connection between two numbers or objects. For example, the relationship between quarters and dollars is that four quarters are equal to one dollar.

repeated doubling To add the same number to itself a specific number of times or to multiply the number by 2 over and over. For example, $7 + 7 + 7 + 7 = 28$ or $7 \times 2 = 14$, $14 \times 2 = 28$.

right angle The space at the vertex where two lines or edges meet to make a square corner.

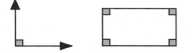

right rectangular prism A prism that has 6 faces, 12 edges, and 8 vertices. All edges form right angles where they meet at the vertices. See the diagram for *prism*.

right triangular prism A prism that has 5 faces, 9 edges, and 6 vertices. There are two congruent right-angled triangles at opposite ends of the prism. See the diagram for *prism*.

round To replace a number with the closest number that ends in 0. For example, the number 76 rounds up to the number 80 because there are five or more ones in the number 76. The number 74 rounds down to the number 70 because there are fewer than five ones in the number 74.

scale The numbers that label the lines on a graph.

strategy A plan (method) that can help solve problems.

subtract To find the difference between two numbers. For example, $150 - 25 = 125$.

symbol A letter, sign, or picture used to represent a word or a group of words. For example, the sign > represents the words *greater than* when comparing two numbers, as in $9 > 6$.

table An organized method to display data.

Kind of Pizza	Number of Orders
Pepperoni	21
Bacon	12
Pineapple	35
Cheese	10

tally chart A chart that uses tally marks to record data.

Colour	Tally Results	Total
Blue	||||	4
Red	卌	5
Yellow	卌 |	6

translate To change from one form of representation to another form of representation. For example, the number form of the pattern 1, 2, 4, 7, 11 can be translated into a visual representation.

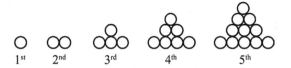

Venn diagram A diagram that uses circles to show relationships among sets. Used for sorting. For example, the numbers 2, 6, 8, 10, 11, 18, 19, 37, and 43 are sorted into 2-digit numbers or even numbers. The numbers in the overlapped area belong to both sets.

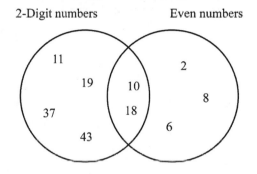

vertex The place where edges meet together on a three-dimensional solid to form corners or points. See diagram for *edge*.

vertical Straight up and down.

whole number Any number made of the digits 0 to 9. For example, 393, 1 549.

written form Any number written in words. For example, the number 4 326 written in words is *four thousand three hundred twenty-six*.

NOTES

BOOK ORDERING INFORMATION
ELEMENTARY and JUNIOR HIGH TITLES

Castle Rock Research offers the following resources to support Alberta students. You can order any of these materials online at:

www.castlerockresearch.com/store

SOLARO - Online Learning		The KEY	SNAP	Prob Solved	Class Notes
$29.95 ea.*		$29.95 ea.*	$29.95 ea.*	$19.95 ea.*	$19.95 ea.*
English Language Arts 9	English Language Arts 6	English Language Arts 9	Science 9	Science 9	Science 9
English Language Arts 8	English Language Arts 5	English Language Arts 6	Mathematics 9	Mathematics 9	Mathematics 9
English Language Arts 7	English Language Arts 4	English Language Arts 3	Mathematics 8	Mathematics 8	Mathematics 8
Mathematics 9	English Language Arts 3	Mathematics 9	Mathematics 7	Mathematics 7	Mathematics 7
Mathematics 8	Mathematics 6	Mathematics 8	Mathematics 6		
Mathematics 7	Mathematics 5	Mathematics 7	Mathematics 5		
Science 9	Mathematics 4	Mathematics 6	Mathematics 4		
Science 8	Mathematics 3	Mathematics 4	Mathematics 3		
Science 7	Science 6	Mathematics 3			
Social Studies 9	Science 5	Science 9			
Social Studies 6	Science 4	Science 6			
	Science 3	Social Studies 9			
		Social Studies 6			

*Prices do not include taxes or shipping.

Study online using **SOLARO,** with access to multiple courses available by either a monthly or an annual subscription.

The KEY Study Guide is specifically designed to assist students in preparing for unit tests, final exams, and provincial examinations.

The **Student Notes and Problems (SNAP) Workbook** contains complete explanations of curriculum concepts, examples, and exercise questions.

The **Problem Solved** contains exercise questions and complete solutions.

The **Class Notes** contains complete explanations of curriculum concepts.

If you would like to order Castle Rock resources for your school, please visit our school ordering page:

www.castlerockresearch.com/school-orders/